The Power of the 8Fs

No 48737 (Darlington 1945 as LNER 'O6' No 3132) features in this footplate view of the southern approach to Winsor Hill Tunnel, just north of Shepton Mallet on the Somerset & Dorset route, on 15 September 1964. The photographer had been granted a footplate pass for the 11.0am freight from Bath to Evercreech Junction and back, this photograph being taken early on the return journey. *Ivo Peters*

The Power of the 8Fs

Jeff Ryan, David McIntosh and George Moon

OPC

An imprint of
Ian Allan Publishing

Contents

First published 2006

ISBN (10) 0 86093 594 X
ISBN (13) 978 0 86093 594 7

© Ian Allan Publishing Ltd 2006

Published by Oxford Publishing Co

an imprint of Ian Allan Publishing Ltd, Hersham, Surrey KT12 4RG
Printed in England by Ian Allan Printing Ltd, Hersham, Surrey KT12 4RG

Code: 0603/A3

Visit the Ian Allan Publishing website at www.ianallanpublishing.com

Introduction

Following the favourable reception given to our previous book *Working Steam: Stanier 8Fs* we were invited by our publisher to provide a similar contribution to the 'Power' series. One review of our earlier book commented on its lack of technical information or a drawing. This was not the intention, nor is it the object of this volume. In both cases we are providing a pictorial record of the life and times of an outstanding class, with extended and informative captions to the photographs. Those seeking technical information or detailed histories of the eventful careers of these engines are referred to the Bibliography. Having said that, we have included in this volume a Glossary dealing with a number of technical terms appearing in the captions; these refer to railway operations in general rather than the '8F' class in particular. We hope you enjoy the journey as we consider the Stanier '8F' 2-8-0 freight locomotive, a type built in greater numbers than almost any other British design and certainly the most widely travelled.

When William Stanier became Chief Mechanical Engineer of the LMS in 1932 much of the heavy freight haulage was in the hands of a large fleet of 0-8-0s (some of ex-LNWR and ex-L&Y pre-Grouping vintage), with well over 700 of these ageing engines in service. The only major

Half title:
The style of cabside numbering applied to Bolton-allocated No 48652 (Eastleigh 1943) is evidence of a visit to Darlington Works as the locomotive waits for the road west with a Class 9 local trip at Manchester Exchange station on 10 June 1968. Sadly, it was performing one of its final duties for withdrawal came later the same month. The photographer is standing at the opposite end of the famous Platform 11, at the extreme western end of Exchange station. Note the collection of platform barrows required for the loading of night-time newspaper trains and parked out of the way during daytime. Manchester Exchange station closed on 5 May 1969. *R. Elsdon*

Title page:
Built by Vulcan Foundry in 1936, LMS No 8042 was a much-travelled '8F'. Requisitioned by the War Department in 1941, becoming WD No 596 it saw overseas service in Iran, as Iranian State Railways No 41.207. Renumbered again in 1944 as WD No 70596, the locomotive was one of 23 '8Fs' acquired by Israel in 1948.
National Railway Museum

freight-locomotive types the LMS had produced were the 33 Beyer-Garratts for mineral haulage on the Midland Division and 175 'Austin Seven' Class 7F 0-8-0s, mainly for use on the Western and Central Divisions, which had been completed by mid-1932. Both classes had serious maintenance problems resulting from their Midland ancestry, inadequate axle-boxes or short-travel valves (or a disastrous combination of both) having been insisted upon by the Derby drawing office. In 1930 the 103 '7Fs' in service recorded 53 'hot boxes' — an appalling record. The ex-LNWR and ex-L&Y 0-8-0s were sturdier, with adequate bearings; indeed, the LNWR variant (the 'G2') was to outlive the newer Fowler '7F'. The new designs had already proved incapable of dealing with the gradual acceleration of freight trains required by the Operating Department; however, the new Stanier 2-8-0 demonstrated an immediate and obvious advance over its '7F' predecessor in terms of reliability, as well as being better-riding, whilst the considerable increase in drawbar horsepower enabled significantly heavier trains to be run at higher speeds.

The importance of freight to the LMS is indicated by the statistics for the economically depressed year of 1934, freight accounting for 58% of receipts, with coal alone representing no less than 20% of that total. By this time the LMS was running 15,000 freight trains every weekday, but 12 years after its formation the company had yet to produce a thoroughly reliable and versatile heavy-freight locomotive.

Stanier's first thoughts for heavy-freight motive power were greatly influenced by the GWR '28xx' 2-8-0 design. Although the original design dated from 1903, its basic strength (and the incorporation of subsequent advances) allowed it to remain in production until 1942. The design was very wide over the cylinders making use of the more generous clearances available on the GWR, which made it unacceptable to the more restricted LMS. Between 1932 and 1934 Stanier's chief draughtsman, T. F. Coleman, had made changes to remove any last vestiges of the '28xx' design. The boiler centre line had to be raised to keep the firebox foundation ring clear of the driving axlebox guides, while the boiler was mounted further forward (by 2ft) to avoid the 'back-end-heavy' appearance of the '28xx'. The characteristically neat and balanced 'Stanier look' of both the 'Black Five' and '8F' owes much to Coleman's work.

The arrival of the new '7F' (soon to be uprated to '8F') 2-8-0s filled a gaping void in the fleet — and with great distinction. The straightforward two-cylinder design made maintenance easy, whilst a maximum axle loading of 18 tons on the tender and only 16 tons on the locomotive allowed the '8Fs' wide route availability. Their free-running capabilities were quickly recognised; they performed well over the whole range of freight duties, tackling express goods and parcels trains with ease and comfortably handling occasional passenger work where speeds in the sixties were frequently recorded. The 2-8-0 wheel arrangement gave better riding and was kinder to the track than its 0-8-0 predecessors. The combination of eight-coupled 4ft 8½in driving wheels, two 18½in x 28in cylinders with 10in-diameter long-travel valves, a well-proportioned free-steaming boiler and excellent front-end design, allied to an all-up weight in working order of 125¾ tons (of which some 63 tons was available for adhesion) and a tractive effort of 32,438lb, proved to be a very sound one. Their ability to negotiate a 4½-chain curve at slow speed was a useful asset on lightly laid foreign metals during World War 2. The engines proved themselves to be equally at home moving 1,000-ton loads of coal to the Home Counties as taking day-trippers to the seaside.

The '8F' class was to have a long production run, becoming one of the few types to have operated on all four

main railways in the UK. It was certainly the only type to
have been constructed by all of the companies, in eight
different workshops and by three contractors, as follows:
Crewe (137), Horwich (75), the GWR at Swindon (80),
the LNER at Doncaster (50) and Darlington (53), the
Southern at Ashford (14), Brighton (93) and Eastleigh (23)
and contractors North British (208), Beyer Peacock (50)
and Vulcan Foundry (69). Of the 852 '8F' locomotives
built, a total of 666 were ultimately to work on British
Railways. The '8F' became the largest class of Stanier
locomotive and the fourth largest class of British
locomotives. The 1,694 'Black Fives' and '8Fs' represented
more than half of the total Stanier locomotives and brought
about a degree of successful standardisation rarely seen on
Britain's railways.

Although only 126 locomotives had been built by 1939,
the '8F' was selected as the first War Department standard
design for overseas service. Ultimately 205 locomotives
reached foreign shores, arriving in Egypt, Iran (Persia) and
Turkey; a further 23 were lost at sea. Many of the Iranian
locomotives (including No 48773) worked on the
formidable 'back-door' supply route to Russia between the
Persian Gulf and Tehran, the changeover point with
Russian forces, *en route* to the Caspian Sea. Prolonged and
heavy gradients made oil-firing essential. The locomotives
supplied to Turkey in 1941 (during which seven were lost
at sea) and 1943 represented the part-fulfilment of a
commercial export order and were assembled in Turkey
under the supervision of LMS engineer Ron Jarvis (who
later was responsible for the reconstruction of the SR
Bulleid Pacifics). As operational needs changed and peace
was declared, the overseas '8Fs' spread considerably. They
eventually saw service in Egypt, Iran, Iraq, Israel, Italy, the
Lebanon, Palestine and Turkey. In time 45 engines returned
to the UK — 39 from the Middle East in 1948, a further
five in 1952 and one from Turkey in 1989. The 1952
shipment included the now preserved No 48773, one of
three which would be taken into BR stock in 1957
following many years of military service. The 1989 returnee
was WD No 348, latterly TCDD (Turkish Railways)
No 45160, which was purchased by the Churchill 8F
Locomotive Co Ltd. The placing of orders, details of
construction and requisition of engines on behalf of the
WD (followed by their peacetime distribution) is a
complex story fully recorded in J. W. P. Rowledge's
Heavy Goods Engines of the War Department (Volume 2),
as listed in the Bibliography.

Meanwhile, at home, the Ministry of War Transport had
faced an increasingly serious shortage of freight locomotives
in 1941/2. Because of its wide route availability, proven
performance and reliability under adverse circumstances,

Stanier's 2-8-0 was selected as the standard wartime freight
locomotive. The LMS itself placed an order for an
additional 205 engines fulfilled by the works at Crewe,
Horwich and North British between 1941-5; a further 245
'8Fs' were built by the other three railway companies
between 1943 and 1945, emerging from Ashford,
Brighton, Darlington, Doncaster, Eastleigh and Swindon.
Most of the 'foreign'-built engines were loaned initially to
the railway companies that had constructed them (with the
exception of the SR), though all were recorded officially as
LMS stock. The LNER also ordered a further 68
locomotives for its own use as Class O6, built at Brighton,
Darlington and Doncaster. Subsequently these were
transferred to the LMS as part of an exchange for surplus
'WD' 2-8-0s.

The '8Fs' lasted well; of the 666 locomotives displaying a
BR number, 638 were still in service in early 1965. At the
end of steam in 1968 more than half of the surviving
locomotives were '8Fs'. The honour of hauling the very last
BR regularly scheduled steam-hauled freight fell to
Swindon-built No 48423, between Preston and Rose Grove
on the evening of Friday 2 August 1968.

The inclusion of David McIntosh in the editorial team
has been beneficial in several ways. A career railwayman for
over 40 years, David began on the footplate in Wales before
Dr Beeching's closures prompted a spell at University.
Returning to BR in 1968 as a graduate trainee he enjoyed a
varied career, mainly in freight operations, with postings in
the West Midlands and at Wakefield, on the staff of the
Director of Operations at the BRB and as Area Manager,
Northwich. Then came a move into business management
of newspaper and mail contracts, followed by a final
10 years in Birmingham and Nottingham with Regional
Railways. Since 1995 he has been a partner in Railway
Consultancy Ltd, specialising in freight projects and
studies. David's wide experience and extensive collection
of Working Timetables and other operating publications
relevant to the eras covered have been put to good use
throughout this volume.

Research for this book has also been enhanced by the
Stanier 8F Locomotive Society's purchase in 2004 of a
complete set of Engine Record Cards from Andrew
Biwandi. The availability of the cards for all 666 BR-owned
'8Fs' has proved useful in a number of respects, although
not all events are recorded on all of the cards. An example
of this research concerns the occasions when '8Fs' were
involved in the working of the Royal Train, where the cards
have confirmed some details. The 'Royal 8Fs', Nos 48309
and 48707, both visited Crewe works in June 1955 for the
fitting of carriage-warming apparatus (CWA) prior to
hauling a Royal Train from Aberystwyth to Milford Haven
on 8 August. From official records, standby No 48330
does not appear to have visited works or had CWA fitted.
There was an earlier Royal duty on 26 October 1952 (from
Llandovery to Milford Haven) also involving No 48309,
with No 48707 as standby, but no works visit is officially
recorded, preparation and fitting of CWA presumably
being undertaken locally at Swansea (Paxton Street). As an
'unofficial' modification it would probably have been
removed before any subsequent works visit and refitted by

Left:
Working a special train of imported steel coil from Birkenhead Docks to the steel terminal at Oldbury & Bromford Lane, a very grimy Birkenhead-allocated No 48326 (Crewe 1944) coasts along the Wolverhampton–Birmingham Stour Valley line through Tipton Owen Street station and towards Watery Lane crossing on 2 May 1964. In 1984 this became the site of Sandwell & Dudley park-and-ride station. *Michael Mensing*

the shed upon return! On the other hand, in his book *Working with LMS Steam* (Bradford Barton 1983) author H. C. H. Burgess (at the time Shedmaster at Paxton Street) states that all three '8Fs' were selected to work the Royal Train (because of their low mileage since their last Works overhaul) and all went to Crewe Works to be fitted with CWA. Only No 48309 is shown retaining CWA throughout its life, but again the author states that 'We now had an additional three engines fitted with CWA for passenger-train working during the steam-heating season. The 2-8-0 "8F" could easily keep time with passenger trains over the Central Wales, and they were invaluable when eight special sleeping-car trains were laid on to convey supporters of the Welsh rugby team from Swansea Victoria to Edinburgh during that winter.'

Stanier '8Fs' penetrated almost every part of the country. From their introduction they dominated freight operations in the Midlands until replaced by diesels in the mid-1960s. During World War 2 they operated over all the Big Four railways and could be seen hauling their vital cargoes to all parts of the mainland. In BR days the majority worked on the London Midland Region, but allocations to all but the Southern meant that they could be seen as far north as Perth, as far east as Norwich and Cambridge, as far west as Plymouth and as far south as Bournemouth and Southampton. The majority of photographs featured in this volume were taken in the BR era and reflect as far as possible the geographical diversity and the wide variety of trains and traffic on which they found employment. The passenger workings shown do, however, over-represent the actual level of traffic handled.

Photographs appearing in this book come from a number of sources. The authors made two visits to the Ian Allan Library and the Stephenson Locomotive Society archive at Hersham and enjoyed a very pleasant afternoon in Wiltshire viewing the '8F' photographs taken by Ivo Peters (through the kindness of his son Julian). Several visits were also made to the continually expanding Kidderminster Railway Museum archive, where the help of David Postle and his colleagues was much appreciated; extensive use has also been made of the 8F Society's photographic collection. Individual Society members have

also contributed significantly in various ways, especially Robin Cullup, Stewart Currie, Rob Newman and Mike Shackleton. In particular special mention must be made of Peter Groom, who has provided invaluable assistance to this project. We have also drawn heavily on the notes provided by the many photographic contributors to this volume. On a number of occasions this extended to direct contact with individuals, either to make a specific request for material or to clarify information. Without fail, this always proved extremely valuable, and it is a pleasure to acknowledge the assistance freely given. To all our photographers we express our very grateful thanks.

As far as possible, photographs that have appeared in earlier Ian Allan '8F' publications have been excluded, but some element of repetition is inevitable, given that almost four decades have passed since the official 'End of Steam'. In preparing captions we have followed our earlier practice of including details of the builder and year of construction of each locomotive featured. Allocations quoted reflect the shedplate carried or contemporary documents. The spelling of place names is that appropriate at the time individual photographs were taken. Within the UK photographs are generally arranged in geographical areas or by route, the exception being the ICI Hoppers. It was the performance of '8Fs' on these limestone workings that led directly to the formation of the Stanier 8F Locomotive Society and the purchase of No 48773, the first '8F' to be preserved.

No 48773 was acquired direct from BR service at the end of regular steam operations in August 1968, a move inspired by the exclusion of a Stanier '8F' from the National Collection. Having worked on six railways on three continents, No 48773 now leads a very active life on the Severn Valley Railway, as well as enjoying occasional main-line outings to locations as diverse as Carlisle and Penzance. The Society is proud of the locomotive's designation as an Official Memorial to the military railwaymen of the Corps of Royal Engineers who fell in World War 2. A very special ceremony took place at Kidderminster in November 2002, when the Chief Royal Engineer, Lieutenant General Sir Scott Grant KCB, dedicated a Roll of Honour recording the details of more than 350 Railway Sappers who died in the conflict.

The year 2005 was also a special one for the Society, the locomotive reaching its 65th 'birthday' and the nation marking the 60th anniversary of the end of World War 2. To commemorate these events No 48773 reverted to its original identity as WD No 307, as turned out by the North British Locomotive Co in Glasgow in June 1940. (The engine is featured as WD No 307 towards the end of this volume.) Its final official appearance in this livery was scheduled for Remembrance Sunday (13 November) 2005, but a return to BR livery was subsequently deferred until after the Christmas running season. The locomotive continues to lead a very active life and by mid-October 2005 had covered 137,729 miles since purchase in 1968. In terms of mileage covered this puts No 48773 in the top echelon of standard-gauge 'heritage' locomotives and is a remarkable tribute to the skills of the men at Bridgnorth MPD. The '8F' story rolls on, seven decades after the type's introduction.

The Survivors section features photographs of most UK-based '8Fs' that have turned a wheel since official withdrawal from service (although not all of the engines listed below fall into this category). WD No 348 (North British 1940), which served in Turkey from 1941 as TCDD No 45160, was privately purchased by the Churchill 8F Locomotive Co and returned to the UK on 14 June 1989, arriving at Immingham on board the *Vikingland*. Originally shipped from Liverpool in January 1941 as part of an export order, this locomotive was one of the 20 '8Fs' dubbed 'Churchills' by Turkish enginemen. Having steamed for a brief period at Swanage soon after return to the UK, it is now on the Gloucestershire–Warwickshire Railway, based at Toddington, where it is currently nearing the end of a prolonged overhaul. In 2005 the owners kindly loaned the Westinghouse pump and two air reservoirs (originally fitted in 1940) to No 48773 to assist in the latter's aforementioned reversion to its original identity as WD No 307.

Starting in 1964, the Woodham Bros scrapyard at Barry played host to six withdrawn '8Fs'. The first to leave was No 48431 (Swindon 1944), in 1972, when a new life beckoned on the Keighley & Worth Valley Railway. The second escapee was No 48151 (Crewe 1942) in 1975, via the Yorkshire Dales Railway and Wakefield to Steamtown at Carnforth, where it now enjoys a very active main-line career. In 1981 No 48624 (Ashford 1943) left Barry for Peak Rail, Buxton; subsequently relocated to Darley Dale, it was last steamed in 1965 but is now nearing the end of an extended overhaul. Since leaving Barry in 1985 No 48305 (Crewe 1943) has spent the bulk of its time on the Great Central Railway but has latterly made a number of appearances elsewhere. The 200th locomotive to escape from Barry was No 48173 (Crewe 1943). Moved to Bitton on the Avon Valley Railway in September 1988, this engine currently awaits restoration. A different fate awaits No 48518 (Doncaster 1944), the only LNER-built '8F' still extant. Its future was determined late in 2004, when custodians Vale of Glamorgan Council, in conjunction with the Heritage Lottery Fund, agreed that the boiler of No 48518 and the frames of Hawksworth 'Modified Hall' 4-6-0 No 7927

Willington Hall should be combined by the Great Western Society to create a new locomotive, No 1014 *County of Glamorgan*. The '8F' is currently resident at the Wales Railway Centre, Barry, but plans are being formulated to move the boiler to Didcot.

Overseas, around six '8Fs' are thought to survive in Turkey, including TCDD Nos 45161 (WD No 522) on display at Camlik Museum and 45168 (WD No 340) at Alasekir. In Iraq one was rediscovered in Baghdad in 2003, not long after the Allied invasion; the current position of any survivors in Iran remains unclear. Finally, two of the 23 lost at sea have recently been positively identified as WD Nos 370 and 371 (both North British 1941). Deck cargo on the sunken World War 2 casualty *SS Thistlegorm* (now a popular site for scuba divers), they are much photographed on the bed of the Red Sea.

Readers interested in receiving details of the Stanier 8F Locomotive Society are invited to contact the Membership Secretary, Peter Stych, at 73 Maesquarre Road, Betws, Ammanford, Carmarthenshire, SA18 2LF (tel: 01269 594865) or to visit the Society's website (www.8fsociety.co.uk). Membership is diverse and includes a number of railwaymen, both civilian and military. New members are always welcome. Members receive *Black Eight*, an excellent A4-size magazine covering a variety of topics and which normally runs to 48 pages. Please feel free to use the above address (or website) for any observations on this book or for other contact with the Society.

Once again we must record our appreciation to our families — Beryl Jones, Sandra Moon and Rosemary, Katherine and Charlotte Ryan. All merit our grateful thanks for their patience, support and understanding, but special thanks must go to Katherine for her computer skills.

Jeff Ryan, David McIntosh and George Moon
for and on behalf of The Stanier 8F Locomotive Society Ltd
November 2005

BIBLIOGRAPHY

Engines of the LMS by J. W. P. Rowledge (Oxford Publishing Co, 1975)

Heavy Goods Engines of the War Department (Volume 2): The Stanier 8F 2-8-0
by J. W. P. Rowledge (Springmead Railway Books, 1977)

Middle East Railways by Hugh Hughes (Continental Railway Circle, 1981)

What Happened to Steam (Volume 28): The LMS 8F 2-8-0s and Somerset & Dorset 7F 2-8-0s by P. B. Hands (published by the author, 1982)

Working with LMS Steam by H. C. H. Burgess (D. Bradford Barton, 1983)

The Railways of Palestine and Israel by Paul Cotterell (Tourret Publishing, 1984)

Great Preserved Locomotives No 1: Stanier 8F No 8233 by Alan Wilkinson (Ian Allan, 1984)

Stanier '8Fs' At Work by Alan Wilkinson (Ian Allan, 1986)

Allied Military Locomotives of the Second World War by R. Tourret (Tourret Publishing, 1995)

Glossary

Wagon types

Bogie Bolster — bogie steel-carrying wagons, the most common type being the 30-ton BBC. The 42-ton BBD was a longer variant. Both 'C' and 'D' types could be fitted or unfitted. The most modern was the 32-ton BBE version, a shorter design for carrying heavy billets. All of the BBE fleet were vacuum-fitted (as was the BBH type).

Carflat — bogie car-carrying wagon, mostly conversions from old passenger-carriage underframes.

Conflat — four-wheel traditional vacuum-fitted container-carrying wagon. Most common type was the Conflat A, which carried 5-ton 'BD' containers. The Conflat L type was designed to convey small, 4-ton-capacity 'L'-type containers for steel-making lime, carried three per wagon. (Conventional containers came in two main variants — the general-use 'BD' and the insulated 'FM' type, the latter painted light blue and used for meat.)

Covhop — four-wheel 24-ton-capacity covered hopper wagon used for bulk powders.

Hopper — bottom-door discharge wagon.

Hyfit or FHG (fitted high goods) — four-wheel open five-plank wagon for general merchandise, often with 'hybar' to support protective tarpaulin wagon sheet. There were variants with both steel and wooden bodies.

Lowfit — four-wheel low-sided wagon designed for vehicular loads, rather than containers. Most often seen in 1960s loaded with agricultural plant, invalid car or MoD vehicle.

Minfit — vacuum-brake-fitted mineral wagon.

Presflo — pressure-discharge wagon for bulk powders (*e.g.* cement).

Prestwin — BR-design pressure-discharge wagon with twin tanks for fine powders (*e.g.* sand).

Tippler — mineral wagon designed to be discharged by upending or rotating (tippled); no side doors, sometimes end doors.

Toad — telegraphic code for an ex-GWR brake van.

Vanfit — four-wheel vacuum-brake-fitted van.

Vanwide — Vanfit with wide doors for palletised traffic.

Departmental wagons
(given 'fish' names — in reality telegraphic codes — by BR)

Catfish — standard 19-ton ballast hopper, centre discharge only.

Dogfish — 24-ton ballast hopper with centre and side discharge.

Grampus — all-purpose side-door-discharge wagon.

Mermaid — side-tipping ballast wagon.

Salmon — BR-design flat-floored bogie wagon for carrying track panels.

Other technical terms

Articulated — bogie vehicles where a bogie is placed between individual vehicles.

Articulated twin set — two coaches with three bogies, articulated at the inner end.

Barrier wagons — empty wagons placed between loaded wagons to provide separation for reasons of overhang or dangerous load.

Block load — a group of wagons conveying the same commodity.

Block train — train formed of a single load from origin to destination.

'Carded' wagon — carrying a 'defective' card: 'Green Card'— may run but for repairs when unloaded; 'Red Card' — not to go forward, requires immediate repairs.

Co-acting — the correct term for semaphore signal arms repeating indications of lower arms, usually for improved visibility from a distance.

Fitted head — a group of vacuum-fitted vehicles attached behind the locomotive at the 'head of train' to give brake force, in addition to the locomotive and to safely allow faster speed for the train.

Part-fitted and fully fitted — trains fitted in part or in full with vacuum brakes, connected to the locomotive and in use.

Piped (sometimes known as a 'blow through') — through vacuum pipe but not fitted.

Speedfreight — fast overnight freight service (indicated in the working timetable by a 'Maltese Cross' symbol), to which accelerated timing applied and to which only XP-coded vehicles could be attached; BR's successor to the LNER's 'Green Arrow' service, it later became 'Speedlink' and is now the EWS 'Enterprise'.

Unfitted — train with no continuous brakes (braking by the locomotive and guard's van only); wagon with no automatic brake (*i.e.* hand brake only).

Train headcodes

In June 1962 BR changed from alphabetical headcodes to a four-character system of train identification in which the first numeric digit denoted the train classification. This table gives a simplified guide to the two systems, changes made when moving to the numerical system being shown in brackets.

Pre-1962	Post-1962	Train description
A	1	Express passenger, newspaper or breakdown train going to clear the line
B	2	Ordinary passenger train, breakdown train not going to clear the line
C	3	Parcels, fish, fruit, livestock, milk or other perishable train formed of XP-classified stock; express freight piped throughout, at least half fitted; empty coaching stock
D	4	Express freight with not less than one-third fitted (Class 4 90%) and piped to the locomotive;
	5	express freight with automatic brake operative on no fewer than half of the vehicles
E	6	Express freight with not less than four (Class 6 20%) fitted vehicles; express freight with limited load, not fitted
F	7	Express freight, livestock, perishable or ballast not fitted with continuous brakes
G	0	Light engine with not more than two brake vans
H	8	Through freight or ballast not running under C, D, E or F conditions, not fitted
J	8	Mineral or empty wagon train, not fitted
K	9	Pick-up or branch freight, mineral or ballast train

Right:
In this view from *c*1937 Toton-allocated No 8045 (Vulcan Foundry 1936) heads north along the Midland main line near Irchester with a very long mixed freight. *H. Gordon Tidey*

Below right:
Electrification of the Woodhead route was halted by World War 2 and only finally completed by BR in 1954. In August 1945 the part-completed structures are prominent as Gorton-allocated No 8532 (Doncaster 1945), only four months old, descends from Woodhead towards Crowden with a train mainly comprising loaded coke wagons. The Gorton-allocated '8Fs' were transferred to Immingham in May 1946, returning to the LMS in October. *W. Potter / Kidderminster Railway Museum*

Below:
Traditional West Coast heavy-freight power, in the form of ex-LNWR 'Super D' No 9352, assists the new order in the form of Toton-allocated No 8006 (Crewe 1935) with northbound Willesden–Toton coal empties approaching Bushey *c*1937. The first 10 wagons are some of the 30 40-ton-capacity hoppers built by the LMS in 1929 to supply the ex-LNWR Stonebridge Park power station. This supplied power for the London-area LM electric services until 1967 and is now the site of the Bakerloo Line depot. *LCGB / Ken Nunn collection*

Above:
The 'Big Freeze' of early 1947 is featured in this newspaper photograph, believed to have been taken at Desford on the Coalville–Leicester line. A three-coach local hauled by an ex-Midland Railway 0-6-0T has come to grief and is being rescued by an unidentified '8F'. *Leicester Mercury*

Left:
In June 1947 Heaton-allocated LNER 'O6' No 3536 (Darlington 1946) accelerates south between Darlington and Croft with a lengthy mixed freight for York. The exhaust suggests coal of poor quality, but the safety valves show a 'white feather' indicating a locomotive easily maintaining full pressure. Renumbered under the LNER scheme from 3136 to 3536 on 2 March 1947, the locomotive is seen with its original number on the smokebox but displaying its new number on the buffer-beam and cabsides. Renumbered 8741 upon transfer to the LMS in September 1947, it later became BR No 48741. *Stanier 8F Society collection*

Above

On 29 July 1947 another Heaton-allocated 'O6', No 3548 (Doncaster 1945), undergoes servicing at York shed. The coal bunker above the locomotive has just been replenished from the now empty wagon being lowered on the left.

Delivered as No 3148, the locomotive became No 3548 on 20 April 1947 under the LNER renumbering scheme; it was renumbered 8753 upon transfer to the LMS at Crewe (and then Swansea) in October 1947 and later became BR No 48753. *C. C. B. Herbert*

Right:

The first Swindon-built '8F', No 8400 (June 1943), was turned out without smokebox numberplate, the number being painted GWR-style on the front buffer-beam. On 6 July 1946 the 'Hall' 4-6-0 heading the 7.10am Paddington–Birmingham Snow Hill failed at Leamington and No 8400 was commandeered from a freight to work the train forward. In this view No 8400 waits at Snow Hill to return light-engine to its home shed at Tyseley. Note (on the right) the SR stock forming a Wolverhampton–Weymouth service. As BR No 48400 the '8F' returned to the WR in 1957 and stayed until 1964. *V. R. Webster / Kidderminster Railway Museum*

Scotland, Carlisle and the West Coast Main Line to Lancaster

Below:
Photographs of '8Fs' in Scotland are comparatively rare, as are pictures taken on the Heads of Ayr branch. In May 1961 the photographer captured both subjects as No 48536 (Doncaster 1945), based at Carlisle (Kingmoor), hauls a weed-killing special deep in Burns country off the Doon Viaduct at Alloway. The Heads of Ayr branch closed as a through route to Girvan in 1955 but was retained for special passenger trains to the Butlins camp at Heads of Ayr until September 1968. *Derek Cross*

Left:
On 17 August 1960 long-time Carlisle (Canal and Kingmoor) resident No 48758 (Doncaster 1945 as LNER 'O6' No 3153) approaches Beattock Summit (1,015ft above sea level) with a Class E train of empty 16-ton mineral wagons heading south from Ravenscraig steelworks in Motherwell and destined for reloading with steel-making lime at Hardendale Quarry, Shap. The 19 Minfits forming the fitted head have apparently yet to carry their first load of lime, unlike the ironstone tipplers at the rear. *Peter Groom*

Right:
October 1964 saw the mass withdrawal of the surviving 'Coronation' Pacifics, the majority of which, along with the earlier withdrawals, were cut up at Crewe. However, eight Carlisle-based examples (shared equally between Kingmoor and Upperby depots) were acquired by the West of Scotland Shipbuilding Co, Troon. In March 1965 a sad cavalcade is pictured at Gretna Green, just beyond Gretna Junction on the GSW route, Leeds (Holbeck)-allocated No 48104 (Crewe 1939) having been borrowed by Kingmoor to work a trip to the breaker's yard with half of the Carlisle contingent. Bringing up the rear is former Upperby resident No 46238 *City of Carlisle. Peter Brock*

Left:
It is nearly midnight on 11 May 1964, and Camden top-link driver Bill Starvis is clearly not having one of his better days as he waits for No 48321 (Crewe 1944), another long-time Kingmoor resident, to be uncoupled from the down 'Caledonian' at Carlisle Citadel station. The '8F' had hauled the train tender-first from Tebay after the second locomotive failure of the trip, an English Electric Type 4 (Class 40) diesel having been replaced at Crewe by a 'Coronation' Pacific which then succumbed at Tebay with injector problems. Arrival at Carlisle was already almost three hours late, the final arrival time at Glasgow (due 11pm) being unrecorded! *Peter Brock*

Left:
The now abandoned goods lines at Carlisle Bog Junction are being used by Newton Heath-allocated No 48200 (North British 1942) in this 1966 view as it coasts towards Rome Street with its special train conveying long-welded rails ready for weekend re-railing operations. The rails were rolled and then cut into 60ft lengths at Workington before being transported to Castleton welding depot, near Rochdale, prior to being moved back north in this special train. Later, the railway was able to supply continuous welded rail direct from source to site, eliminating this double-handling. *Stanier 8F Society collection*

Right:
Having joined the Carlisle goods lines at Carlisle No 13 (Upperby Junction), No 48252 (North British 1941) of Croes Newydd coasts round towards Bog Junction and Carlisle New Yard on 22 July 1967 with the 5.45am Class 5 part-fitted freight from Preston Ribble Sidings to Carlisle. Included in the train, behind five Vanfits and two Hyfits, is a block of Presflo pressure-discharge cement-carrying wagons. Visible in the background (right) is Upperby locomotive shed (12B), closed the previous December. *R. J. Humm*

Above:
A case of '8F' superpower on 6 August 1966 as Nos 48352 (Horwich 1944) and 48471 (Swindon 1945), banked by 2-6-4T No 42665 (a recent arrival at Tebay from a more leisurely life at Southport), storm up Shap near Scout Green with a heavy Class 8 train of prefabricated track panels from Castleton pre-assembly depot near Rochdale. Newton Heath has borrowed Royston's No 48352 to assist its own No 48471 to work this special out-of-gauge load of Salmon wagons. The empty first wagon is provided to accept the first panel of the lifted old track (which will be removed from site by the same train), the old panels simply replacing the new. Note that No 48471 retains the GWR-type vacuum ejector fitted from 1956 to Swindon-built '8Fs' allocated to the Western Region. *Ian S. Carr*

Left:
Sunday engineering work south of Grayrigg on 1 August 1965 sees Mansfield's No 48362 (Horwich 1944) on the up line waiting to position manned Dogfish ballast hoppers for unloading. Alongside, on the down line, No 48222 of Royston (North British 1942) climbs slowly into position to collect spoil from a ballast-cleaning machine, working away noisily behind the photographer. In the distance, behind No 48362's train, is an early design of ballast-tamping machine ready to align and level the track once the new ballast has been dropped. Sunday engineering was always a valid reason for sheds — in this case Carlisle Kingmoor — to borrow foreign locomotives visiting at the weekend. *Derek Cross*

Left:
In the final winter for BR steam, on 20 December 1967, there is frost on the ground as Patricroft-allocated No 48491 (Horwich 1945) storms unassisted up Shap with a 28-wagon mixed freight. Lighting conditions suggest this may be the 6L00 8.33am Walton Old Junction (Warrington)–Carlisle working, due at Tebay at 2.23pm. *L. A. Nixon*

Above right:
The short 1-in-98 climb from Lancaster Castle to Lancaster No 1 Junction (Milepost 1 of the erstwhile Lancaster & Carlisle Railway) has hardly slowed No 48115 (Crewe 1939), heading for home on 12 September 1964 with train 7J93, the 8.42am Carlisle–Patricroft part-fitted freight. *Noel A. Machell*

Right:
Newton Heath-allocated No 48318 (Crewe 1944) coasts through the smart but deserted Garstang & Catterall station on the West Coast main line south of Lancaster on 13 August 1965. The Class 7 Carlisle–Basford Hall (Crewe) freight is loaded mostly with a block load of new pipes behind a Vanfit and a milk tank. The up siding is filled with empty vans, whilst the former Knott End branch (only finally closed from Garstang Town a few weeks earlier, on 19 July) is being used to stable a block load of sheeted Hyfits, possibly waiting shipment from nearby Glasson Dock. *Peter Fitton*

Right:
No 48310 (Crewe 1943) of Rose Grove has a good head of steam and is not bothering to take water from Brock troughs just north of Preston with this 20-coach northbound movement of empty coaching stock at 9.40am on 13 April 1966. The train is formed of two 10-coach sets of LMS design, which were becoming quite rare by this date and were possibly returning to Scotland after forming Easter extras to Blackpool. *Peter Fitton*

Left:
Holbeck-allocated No 48283 (North British 1942) pounds up the 1-in-100 rising grade into Kirkby Stephen station with the heavy southbound (6F40) 9.10am Long Meg–Widnes block load of anhydrite on 28 April 1967. By this date Class 9F 2-10-0 locomotives were predominant. Despite the smoke effects (generated by recent firing) the 'white feather' at the safety valves indicates a free-steaming locomotive fully on top of the task in hand and reassurance for the crew of an easy run over the continuing seven-mile climb to Ais Gill Summit. *Derek Cross*

Below:
Wild Boar Fell towers in the background above Ais Gill Summit as No 48421 (Swindon 1943), a recent transfer from Aintree to Northwich, heads for home with the 4.20pm Larbert–Wallerscote soda-ash empties (5M27) on 29 April 1967.
This working had only recently gone over to diesel haulage, so Control may have decided upon this as a means of getting No 48421 home during a period when diesels were in short supply. *Ivo Peters*

Right:
Approaching Ais Gill behind No 48505 (Darlington 1944) of Crewe South shed, three withdrawn Scottish diesel shunters — North British-built Nos D2752 and D2712 plus (at the rear) Barclay No D2441, all with side rods removed for movement — make a final journey south on 14 September 1967. The train has no brake van, being regarded as three dead locomotives and not a train as such, no guard or van therefore being required. The diesels had been withdrawn from Millerhill and Hamilton and were probably moving south to Booth's yard at Rotherham, where many diesel shunters were scrapped once their engines had been removed for re-sale to industrial users. *J. Scrace*

Left:
Garsdale water troughs were located on one of the few level stretches on the Settle–Carlisle line. In 1959 Holbeck-based No 48443 (Swindon 1944) needs no refreshment as it ambles south with a lightweight freight, probably conveying permanent-way materials recovered during the course of the frequent track maintenance that was necessary in the vicinity of water troughs. *Eric Treacy*

Right:
Curving away just south of Hellifield on 23 April 1965, its distinctive style of cabside numbering evidence of a recent visit to Darlington Works for overhaul, Holbeck's No 48283 (North British 1942) coasts downhill with the 7N54 12.40pm empty ammonia tanks from Heysham to Haverton Hill (Billingham). This working required barrier wagons — in this case two Hyfits — between locomotive and train because of the dangerous nature of the load.
Peter Fitton

Left:
Preston No 5's fine array of semaphores stand witness on 17 January 1968 as Northwich-allocated No 48063 (Vulcan Foundry 1936) gets into its stride with the 7L00 11.15am Oakleigh–Corkickle freight, carrying soda ash in Covhops from ICI Northwich to the Marchon chemical plant at Whitehaven. Six weeks later it was all over, as Northwich shed closed to steam and Class 40 diesels took over the train. The Marchon plant was located on the top of a hill overlooking Whitehaven, rail access being achieved via the cable-worked 'Corkickle brake' inclined plane. *Ken Horan*

Preston, the Fylde Peninsula, Wigan and East Lancashire

Left:
On 8 October 1965 Lostock Hall's No 48002 (Crewe 1935) departs Platform 8 of the East Lancs (EL) side of Preston station with empty stock for Blackpool, where spare sets of coaches were stabled. Duties for these vehicles no doubt included Illuminations specials, the season running from 3 September to 24 October that year. *Glenn B. Clarkson*

Left:
Edge Hill's No 48433 (Swindon 1944) hauls a Class F block load of Covhops through the busy station at Kirkham & Wesham, *en route* from the ICI Burn Naze plant at Fleetwood to Corkickle, on 14 October 1961. At Preston the train will reverse direction using the Farington Curve, Lostock Hall and Todd Lane junctions, thus passing through Preston twice within 20 minutes in opposite directions. This practice often caused as much confusion to Scotland–Blackpool passengers on through trains as to visiting trainspotters. *Peter Fitton*

Right:
On 11 July 1964 the sunshine and beaches of Blackpool are not far away as Newton Heath-allocated No 48318 (Crewe 1944) crosses from the down fast to the Marton direct line at Kirkham North Junction with the 1T52 excursion from Todmorden to Blackpool Central. Note the use of non-corridor stock without toilets for this journey of two hours plus — often more of a problem on the return trip, after plenty of local liquid refreshment. *Peter Fitton*

Below:
The mills and factories of Leyland fill the background as Newton Heath's No 48471 (Swindon 1945) coasts towards Farington Junction with the 7L00 8.33am Walton Old Junction (Warrington)–Carlisle freight on 20 September 1967. The fitted head is formed of Hyfits loaded with rock salt from the mine at Winsford, loaded at Over & Wharton and *en route* to Scotland for use on winter roads. Note the WR-style vacuum ejector fitted to this one-time WR locomotive. *Peter Fitton*

Above:
On a foggy October morning in 1966 the countryside around Hoghton on the Preston–Blackburn line reverberates to the thunderous exhaust of Sutton Oak's No 48149 (Crewe 1942) as it assists an unidentified '9F' up the 1-in-101 rising grade. The train is a Class 8 heavy load of new prefabricated concrete-sleepered track panels from Castleton, heading north for weekend re-laying work. *B. Walker*

Right:
Late in the evening of 13 June 1968 Rose Grove's No 48393 (Horwich 1945), bearing a chalked 'Farewell to Steam' inscription, coasts downhill at Hoghton towards Lostock Hall with the 4P21 6.40pm Darwen–Heysham empty fuel tanks. *Peter Fitton*

Left:
Hoghton was a favourite photographic location at the summit of the three-mile 1-in-99/101 climb from Bamber Bridge. Here, on 6 April 1968, No 48666 (Brighton 1944) of Rose Grove storms up the last few yards to the summit with the 7N78 8.35am Wyre Dock (Fleetwood)–Healey Mills coal empties. *Paul Claxton*

Below right:
Passing the Lancashire/Yorkshire boundary at Portsmouth on Saturday 18 May 1968, No 48410 (Swindon 1943) of Rose Grove applies maximum effort as it assists yet another load of Yorkshire coal on the climb towards Copy Pit. *B. Lister*

Left:
The end of steam is only two months away as Newton Heath's No 48368 (Horwich 1944) heads west from Rose Grove with a Colne–Preston parcels train on 6 June 1968. Rose Grove shed (10F), one of the last steam sheds to survive, is visible in the background (left). Many former cotton mills in East Lancashire gained a new lease of life handling mail-order-catalogue goods; this service was designed to cater for such traffic, feeding at Preston into a variety of long-distance overnight parcels services. *K. P. Lawrence*

Right:
Rose Grove shed's huge coaling plant dominates the scene on 10 April 1968 as locally allocated No 48257 (North British 1941) heads back to Padiham power station with another Class 9 trip conveying power-station (small) coal. The locomotive carries a miniature snowplough — unlikely to be required in the few months left before the end of steam. More '8Fs' are visible behind the coaling plant and the distinctive L&Y-style Rose Grove West signalbox. Today little trace remains of the shed, yard and signalbox, the current scene being dominated by the M65 motorway. *Paul Cotterell*

Left:
At the north end of York station on 17 August 1961, Willesden's No 48648 (Brighton 1943) is far from home as it leaves the Scarborough line with a Class E part-fitted freight from the Foss Islands branch to Dringhouses yard (York) and Crewe. The ex-'Jubilee' Fowler tender was acquired during a recent visit to Crewe Works for a Light Intermediate overhaul, the '8F' regaining a Stanier tender (from No 48215) in 1966. *P. Fareham*

Left:
Heading south on 10 June 1963 between Bardsey and Thorner on the Wetherby–Cross Gates line, Farnley Junction's No 48664 (Brighton 1944) and Neville Hill's tender-first 'Q6' 0-8-0 No 63420 slowly drag their 63-wagon 1,000-ton train towards the summit just north of Scholes. The load of spent ballast from re-laying work will be taken on to Barlow tip near Selby, following reversal at Neville Hill. *J. M. Rayner*

Left:
No 48352 (Horwich 1944) of Royston shed has come across the ex-GN line from Low Moor and Dudley Hill to arrive at Laisterdyke yard (Bradford) with this Class 8 load of domestic coal from Healey Mills in September 1967. Note the attractive ex-GN East Junction signalbox and the distinctive cabside numbers applied to the locomotive by Darlington Works following a Heavy Intermediate overhaul in August 1965. *M. Dunnett*

Above:
Holbeck's No 48104 (Crewe 1939), fitted with a miniature snowplough, powers round the curve on the down slow at Newlay on the ex-Midland route from Leeds to the North on 10 June 1967. In this second view of the 10.50am Hunslet–Carnforth freight the locomotive is carrying Class 7 lamps. *L. A. Nixon*

Right:
On 1 June 1956 Normanton-based No 48202 (North British 1942) hauls a Class H mixed freight round the Whitehall curve at Leeds and heads for Skipton. On the left ex-LNER Class D49/2 'Hunt' 4-4-0 No 62775 *The Tynedale*, of Leeds (Neville Hill) shed, approaches with a local passenger train from Leeds City to Harrogate. *Eric Treacy*

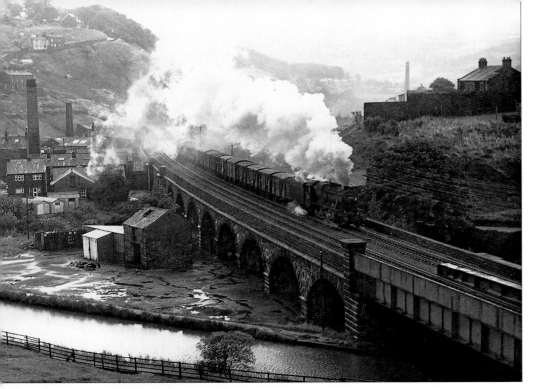

Left:
In driving rain on 5 September 1967 an unidentified '8F' climbs through Gauxholme and prepares to cross the Rochdale Canal south of Todmorden with the 8M94 7.20am Healey Mills–Moston freight. Moston yard, four miles north of Manchester, handled westbound traffic over the Calder Valley route. *C. J. Mills*

Left:
On 28 October 1962 No 48139 (Crewe 1941) of Widnes wheels a Class 8 Mirfield–Garston empty banana-van special up the 1-in-182 rising grade through Todmorden towards Summit Tunnel and the descent to Manchester.
Richard S. Greenwood

Left:
No 48139 again, this time at Hall Royd Junction, where the lines via Copy Pit (left) and Manchester (right) separate. Here, on 13 October 1962, the locomotive is heading a Class 8 mixed freight from Mirfield to Garston. *Richard S. Greenwood*

Left:
Steam reigned supreme on freight work in the Calder Valley, but double-headed trains such as this were rare. Rose Grove's No 48218 (North British 1942) and an unidentified 'WD' 2-8-0 battle through a snowstorm at Eastwood, east of Todmorden, on 27 November 1965. The '8F' was probably being used both for extra adhesion on this Class 8 load of coal and as a means of getting back home. *Richard S. Greenwood*

Right:
On 30 July 1960 a Summer Saturday Midland Division (M7) eight-coach relief to Blackpool offers the opportunity for Class A work to the seaside for long-term Nottingham resident No 48696 (Brighton 1944). The train is clinging to the hillside as it climbs along the Calder Valley towards Eastwood. From the clear exhaust, the fireman has yet to build up his fire ready for the climb to Copy Pit. *Richard S. Greenwood*

Left:
On a distinctly damp winter day, Royston's No 48443 (Swindon 1944) heads an eastbound Class 8 freight towards Mirfield and Healey Mills yard on 26 February 1966. The low-sided ferry wagon behind the locomotive is probably heading back for the Harwich–Zeebrugge train ferry via Healey Mills and Whitemoor. Note that the distant signals for Heaton Lodge Junction are rare examples of splitting colour lights. *Peter Fitton*

Left:
Amidst typical Calder Valley scenery of woollen mills and chimneys, Newton Heath's No 48321 (Crewe 1944) is fully master of the task as it heads west through Elland and towards the tunnel with a 900-ton-plus Class 8 block load of coal on 3 May 1968. *John Hunt*

Left:
In typical West Riding weather in July 1966 Trafford Park's No 48535 (Doncaster 1945) coasts past Mirfield shed (56D). The first wagon on the train is a Vanwide returning to York Foss Islands for another load of palletised Rowntree's chocolate. Visible on shed are Wakefield-allocated 'WD' No 90200, a '9F' 2-10-0, and, on the coal stage, another 'WD' and an '8F'. Note the unique ex-LMS American-style 'speed signals', installed in 1932 and destined to remain in use until 1969. *Ian Krause*

Old and new forms of freight haulage run alongside each other as parallel arrivals from the west approach Healey Mills yard through Thornhill on 1 May 1968. Rose Grove's No 48167 (Crewe 1943), bringing coal empties from East Lancashire for reloading in Yorkshire, is flanked by an unidentified English Electric Type 3 (Class 37) diesel performing a similar function with a train from the Manchester area. *Peter Fitton*

Having been called forward by Kirkgate East signalbox, No 48503 (Darlington 1944) negotiates Wakefield Kirkgate with another load of eastbound coal empties on 16 June 1965. By this date passengers had to find their way amongst the barrows, for the principal role of this ex-L&Y station was by now that of a large parcels depot (although the overall roof would be retained until 1972). A long-term resident at Heaton Mersey, No 48503 owes its smart external appearance on this occasion to a Heavy Intermediate overhaul at Crewe the previous month.
Peter Fitton

Allocated to Newton Heath from May 1964 until withdrawal at the end of 1965, No 48391 (Horwich 1945) heads past Calder Bridge Junction and Wakefield shed (56A) with a Class 7 load of coal empties. Presumably a relief crew took over at Healey Mills to work the train forward to Crofton or Royston for local collieries.
Eric Treacy

Left:
At Goose Hill Junction (Normanton) on 15 August 1966 the last operational 'V2' in England, No 60831 of York, working the 3pm York–Healey Mills freight, stands with the blower hard on as it waits for Holbeck's No 48104 (Crewe 1939) to cross the junction with a Tinsley–Stourton freight. The fourth wagon in this train is a Conflat conveying one of the 'Speedfreight' containers used on the original Hendon–Gushetfaulds (Glasgow) 'Condor' overnight container service.
Peter Fitton

Left:
Also on 15 August 1966 Stourton-allocated No 48093 (Vulcan Foundry 1937) heads westbound coal empties through Normanton station whilst another '8F' waits to go on shed. In the sidings local 2-6-4T No 42149 is waiting to take empty parcels vans to Wakefield and Huddersfield.
Peter Fitton

Left:
A second view of No 48664, here heading a Class H mixed freight through Goole *c*1961, probably *en route* for Leeds via Knottingley. Seen carrying a 55D (Royston) shedplate, the locomotive would be transferred to Farnley Junction in October 1961, returning to Royston in November 1966. *P. Cookson*

Right:
The prevailing gradient on the 10-mile
climb from the Calder Valley to
Standedge Tunnel is 1 in 105.
In 1954 Warrington-allocated
No 48714 (Brighton 1944 for LNER
as 'O6' No 7660) climbs steadily
along the up fast line, passing
Linthwaite Goods with a Class H
mixed freight from Huddersfield
(Hillhouse) to Warrington Arpley.
Eric Treacy

Left:
The last day of operation on the
former Hull & Barnsley Railway was
4 August 1967. The final load of coal
from Brodsworth Colliery to head
west for Cudworth yard arrives at
Wrangbrook Junction behind
Royston's No 48710 (Brighton 1944
for LNER as 'O6' No 7656).
Brodsworth remained rail-served for a
few more years via the ex-GN line.
Peter Fitton

Right:
Northwich-allocated No 48742
(Darlington 1946 as LNER 'O6'
No 3137) coasts into Sheffield
Victoria with a lengthy excursion
train from Manchester to
Cleethorpes. Formed of ex-LNER
stock, including some articulated
vehicles, this has come via the
electrified Woodhead route, on which
engineering work has required the
power to be isolated. The locomotive,
presumably borrowed by Gorton, will
probably be changed here for more
suitable power from Darnall shed for
the next leg through Worksop and
Gainsborough to Cleethorpes.
Stephenson Locomotive Society collection

Manchester and Cheshire

Above:
Smithy Bridge, between Littleborough and Rochdale, has traditionally been the reporting-point between the Manchester and Leeds divisions on the Calder Valley route. Here, coasting downhill on 7 August 1961, Mirfield's No 48608 (Eastleigh 1943) has been borrowed by Low Moor to haul this Bank Holiday Monday excursion (1X28) from Bradford Exchange to Belle Vue in Manchester. The leading ex-LMS non-corridor coaches have no toilet provision, unlike the ex-LNER non-corridor coaches at the rear. *Richard S. Greenwood*

Below:
Typical Lancashire cotton mills form the backdrop to this view between Castleton and Rochdale as Birkenhead's No 48348 (Horwich 1944) heads east with a long Middleton Junction–Healey Mills Class F coal empties on 15 August 1961. *Richard S. Greenwood*

Right:
Edge Hill's No 48249 (North British 1940) pilots Holbeck 'Jubilee' No 45565 *Victoria* with the Scotswood Sidings (Heaton)– Red Bank (Manchester Victoria) empty newspaper vans, passing Castleton sidings on the approach to Manchester on 2 August 1960. This train was usually double-headed and often loaded to more than 20 vans, being the means by which vans were returned to Manchester, having formed several of the previous night's newspaper trains across the Pennines. The express-passenger locomotive would probably return east on similar work. *Richard S. Greenwood*

Right:
Newton Heath station may be gas-lit but still has all its facilities in place on 3 April 1965, shortly before closure on 1 January 1966. With its home shed visible in the background, No 48612 (Ashford 1943) hauls a load of coal north for Chadderton power station. Note that on the up-line signal gantry the distants are colour lights below semaphores, a combination subsequently banned because the brighter colour lights tended to obscure the oil-lit semaphores. *Mike Shackleton*

Right:
Against a pleasant rural background a Sunday excursion from Oldham to Blackpool, assisted as far as Rochdale by Wigan-based 2-6-4T No 42632, coasts in to New Hey station on 31 July 1960. The train engine is an unidentified '8F', while at the front of the consist is an ex-LNER articulated twin-set. *Richard S. Greenwood*

Left:
On 6 June 1967 the guard is busy with his shunting pole, attaching coal empties, as his train calls at Royton Junction. Newton Heath-allocated No 48758 (Doncaster 1945) prepares to draw forward as operations continue. The working was originally believed to be 8J70, the 3.13pm Hollinwood–Moston trip via Oldham Mumps and Rochdale, but subsequent enquiries have revealed that the photograph was taken at 7.15pm. Royton Junction station, behind the photographer, was one mile north of Oldham Mumps. Nowadays only the double-track running-lines remain, passengers using a new station at Derker, slightly nearer to Oldham.
Peter Hutchinson

Below:
At the west end of Standedge Tunnel (summit of the ex-LNW trans-Pennine route) is Diggle, where in the winter of 1962/3 an unidentified Stanier '8F', coupled back-to-back with a 'WD' 2-8-0, is seen engaged on snow-clearance duties. The two locomotives have just come up from Stalybridge over the Micklehurst Loop (closed 1966), which served as the slow lines from Stalybridge on the opposite side of the valley to the surviving line through Greenfield.
J.R Carter

Right:

The appropriately named 'OA&GB Junction' (Oldham, Ashton-under-Lyne and Guide Bridge) was a reminder of the former GCR/LNWR joint line, located just to the east of the Ashton Moss junctions. On 29 August 1964 No 48158 (Crewe 1943), a Holbeck resident since February 1948, was looking rather smart, having emerged from a Heavy Intermediate overhaul at Crewe only 17 days earlier. Arriving from Oldham light-engine, the locomotive would fork left immediately beyond the bridge to Ashton Moss South Junction prior to reversing into Ashton Oldham Road goods yard for an afternoon session of shunting. In the mid-1950s Hornby Dublo selected this locomotive as the prototype for its first '00'-gauge '8F' model. *Mike Shackleton*

Right:

A little further west on this ex-L&Y line, which formed a key link in the ex-LNW Manchester–Leeds route via Standedge, are Clayton Bridge station and level crossing. On 27 April 1968 enthusiasts throng the platform as a joint Severn Valley Railway Society / Manchester Rail Travel Society railtour (1Z77), hauled by Bolton-based No 48652 (Eastleigh 1943), storms through heading for Stockport via Reddish South. Following closure of the station on 7 October 1968 only the level crossing now survives, operated through closed-circuit television from Baguley Fold signalbox. *D. A. Idle*

Right:

On 2 November 1967 a guard walking along Manchester Victoria's Platform 11, which at 2,194ft was famous as Britain's longest (and extended through to Manchester Exchange station), does not even turn his head as Heaton Mersey's No 48765 (Doncaster 1946 as LNER 'O6' No 3160) carefully trundles past westbound on the up through line with a Class 8 mixed freight. The train is at the bottom of the 1-in-47/59 falling gradient from Miles Platting. The Bogie Bolster C, third up behind the locomotive, is flanked by a Lowfit and Conflat because its load of long steel sections overhangs the wagon ends and needs some barrier protection. *John H. Bird*

Above:
Dewsnap Sidings at Guide Bridge principally handled eastbound traffic heading over the Woodhead route. On the left in this early-1960s scene recorded at the entrance to the No 1 group sidings is ex-Midland '3F' 0-6-0 No 43809, based locally at Gorton; drawing its train into No 1 up reception is an unidentified Stanier '8F' 2-8-0 with specialised Conflat L wagons carrying 'L'-type containers for steel-making lime traffic and designed for bottom discharge through holes in the wagon floor. The large building in the background (right) is the erstwhile Dukinfield Carriage Works of the Great Central Railway. *G. Richard Parkes*

Left:
With the ex-MR Marple Wharf Junction in the background, Newton Heath's No 48368 (Horwich 1944) accelerates northwards in April 1968 with a Class 7 mixed freight from Gowhole to Brewery Sidings (Miles Platting), where eastbound traffic over the Calder Valley route was handled. The first wagon is an ex-Southern ballast-plough brake van. *L. A. Nixon*

Above:
On Easter Monday (19 April) 1954 a Bank Holiday excursion (C921) from Low Moor to Longsight (for Belle Vue) arrives at Heaton Norris Junction in the capable hands of Widnes-allocated No 48720 (Brighton 1944 for LNER as 'O6' No 7666). The train will reverse here and be worked forward by another Widnes '8F', No 48753 (Doncaster 1945 as LNER 'O6' No 3148), off the previous arrival, No 48720 following light-engine to Longsight shed. Note the early BR tender emblem on the locomotive and the use of non-corridor, non-toilet-fitted stock on an excursion; also the surviving ex-LNWR tall wooden signals. *Peter Hutchinson*

Above:
Shortly after mid-day No 48338 (Horwich 1944) of Heaton Mersey powers through the deserted platforms of Stockport's Tiviot Dale station with an eastbound haul of coal empties on 23 March 1963. The train is bound for Godley Junction, where an 'EM1' (Class 76) DC electric locomotive will take over for the return journey via the Woodhead route to the Yorkshire Coalfield. *Peter Fitton*

Above:
In the 1950s Longsight shed rostered Stanier '8Fs' on evening commuter trains to Buxton whenever the need arose. One such occasion was Friday 14 August 1959, when No 48680 (Brighton 1943) featured on the 5.50pm Manchester London Road–Buxton passenger service. In this view the train is approaching Davenport, the first stop after Stockport. At least No 48680 has 50% balanced motion and carries the cabside star emblem, indicating suitability for fast freight work.
R. Keeley

Left:
The Stretford End of Manchester United's football ground at Old Trafford forms the backdrop as locally allocated No 48356 (Horwich 1944) trundles empty coal hoppers forward from Trafford Park sidings and alongside the single platform of the Manchester United Football Ground station on 12 September 1967.
John A. M. Vaughan

Above:
Newton Heath's No 48115 (Crewe 1939) sits on the turntable at Patricroft shed (26F) in late August 1961. The locomotive is in ex-works condition after a Heavy General overhaul (including fitting of AWS), completed at Horwich on 18 August, at which time the photographer was a Patricroft fireman. *J.R Carter*

Right:
The local chemical plant dominates this view of Warrington Bank Quay on 27 September 1967 as No 48060 (Vulcan Foundry 1936) of Speke Junction shed coasts through the Low Level station (closed 1958) eastwards towards Arpley Junction with an express freight from Garston to Healey Mills. The High Level platforms survive to this day. *J. H. Cooper-Smith*

Above:
For most of their lives the Wirral electric sets were overhauled at Horwich Works. On 18 April 1967 a newly overhauled set is pictured climbing to the Ship Canal overbridge at Acton Grange *en route* to Birkenhead North depot, hauled by No 48319 (Crewe 1944) of Springs Branch (Wigan). This 'out-of-gauge' Class 8 movement required special barrier wagons because of the air brakes and knuckle couplers fitted to these units. The route from Horwich was via Bolton (reverse), Wigan Wallgate (reverse), Warrington, Mickle Trafford, Dee Marsh and Bidston.
Brian Garvin

Right:
West Cheshire Junction, between Helsby and Stanlow, is where the branch line from Mouldsworth (CLC) joined the Helsby–Hooton route. Just along the branch, the large BICC cable factory enjoyed a service of workers' trains from Birkenhead to the former Helsby & Alvanley station, this continuing well into the 1970s. On 2 February 1957 an '8F'-hauled freight bound for Ince & Elton power station observes the 15mph speed restriction through the junction as a Stanier Class 3 2-6-2T, approaching the junction with its long factory workers' special, is checked before it can cross onto the branch. The signalbox at West Cheshire having burned down, the branch through to Mouldsworth closed to all traffic on 14 September 1991. *Norman Jones*

Right:
On 30 April 1964 Speke Junction's No 48520 (Doncaster 1944) rolls into Runcorn station with a Class 9 local trip from Garston to Runcorn Folly Lane yard. The brake van behind the locomotive is required because the train will have to reverse just south of the station in order to gain access to the Folly Lane branch, which served the large ICI complex at Runcorn and Weston Point Docks. In the background the modern road bridge over the River Mersey (itself a 1960s replacement for the Runcorn–Widnes transporter bridge) dwarfs the original railway bridge. *Peter E. Baughan*

Left:
Just south of Acton Grange Junction (Warrington) on a wintry day in late December 1964 an '8F' heads a fast freight south towards Weaver Junction and passes a northbound freight hauled by a 'Black Five'. *Mike Esau*

Left:
Three types of heavy-freight locomotive feature in this 1966 view of Birkenhead shed (8H), all having been turned to face south in readiness for their next job. On the left is a visitor from Heaton Mersey, No 48199 (North British 1942); centre-stage is locally based one-time Crosti-boilered '9F' (by now officially '8F') 2-10-0 No 92021, while on the right is single-chimney '9F' No 92082. Towards the end of steam Birkenhead had a large stud of '9Fs'. *Ian Allan Library*

Left:
On 20 May 1953 Birkenhead-allocated No 48094 (Vulcan Foundry 1937) rolls into the south end of Crewe station with a long Class J coal train from the Stoke line. The 'independent' lines avoiding Crewe station lacked access from the Stoke line, hence the routeing of this freight through the station. *Peter Hutchinson*

Below:
With the hills of the High Peak above Hayfield visible in the distance and the Peak Forest Canal in the foreground, Warrington's No 48247 (North British 1940) passes New Mills (ex-LNW) with a mixed load of both wooden and steel empty mineral wagons from Buxton on 29 June 1956. *Norman Jones*

The Peak District

Right:
In February 1966 Heaton Mersey-allocated No 48161 (Crewe 1943) gets into its stride on the up slow line away from New Mills South Junction with the 1.25pm Dewsnap–Buxton freight. Note the tall co-acting arms on the down fast home signal (left), provided to aid visibility for trains approaching at speed down the gradient from Chinley. *John R. Hillier*

Below:
A Class 8 trip of loaded coal hoppers from Gowhole yard to Peak Forest sidings approaches Buxworth and provides the opportunity for a spectacular display of smoke and fury in this view from 27 January 1968. Patricroft-allocated No 48775 (Crewe 1937) shows the results of cleaning by enthusiasts, while the crew are entering into the spirit of these last few months of regular main-line steam. The boiler is still fitted with ex-WD clacks (higher than the standard '8F' fittings) requiring a diagonal yellow stripe on the cabside, although none was ever applied! *D. E. Gouldthorp*

Above:
Newton Heath's No 48758 (Doncaster 1946 as LNER 'O6' No 3153) disturbs the tranquillity of Chinley station as it rumbles downhill with the 8F70 11.25am Toton–Garston freight on 29 October 1966. There was still 20 months to go before the main line to Derby via Peak Forest closed and such trains became just a memory. *L. A. Nixon*

Below:
Routed via the up fast line between Chinley station and Chinley North Junction, the driver of No 48348 (Horwich 1944) has decided to mount a lusty charge on the 1-in-90 rising gradient to Peak Forest. His fireman has responded by firing a round to produce these smoke effects as the Birkenhead-allocated locomotive moves empty iron-ore hoppers back to the East Midlands from the Lancashire Steelworks at Irlam on 18 April 1964. *R. J. Farrell*

By 1 May 1968 the last regular steam-hauled freight along the Hope Valley line was the 7.5pm Earle's Sidings–Widnes block load of Presflo wagons, conveying cement. The Class 6 train is pictured between Hope and Edale as Heaton Mersey's No 48723 (Brighton 1944 for LNER as 'O6' No 7669) gets into its stride up the long 1-in-100 climb to Cowburn Tunnel. The milepost (168) on the left is measured from 0 at St Pancras via Leicester and Alfreton. *L. A. Nixon*

Left:
Passing Peak Forest Junction northbound trains still have three miles to climb at 1-in-90 before reaching Peak Forest Summit. In May 1967 the exhaust of Buxton's No 48424 (Swindon 1943) echoes across the valley as the locomotive joins the main line to climb north with a Buxton–Gowhole mixed freight. The first two vehicles are Prestwin pressure-discharge wagons for powdered traffic, of which 130 were built in 1960. Towards the rear is a rake of loaded Mermaid side-tipping ballast wagons. *Derek Cross*

Below left:
On the last day of steam at Buxton (2 March 1968) locally allocated No 48744 (Darlington 1946 as LNER 'O6' No 3139) climbs up to Hindlow, on the former line to Ashbourne, with a Buxton–Briggs Sidings trip. The train is a mixed rake of loaded coal hoppers and lime empties for the quarries set high up in the appropriately named White Peak. *Ian Krause*

Above right:
Against a typical Hindlow background of quarries and kilns, Buxton's No 48442 (Swindon 1944) rolls carefully out of Hindlow Tunnel and down the steep gradient towards home in December 1967 with a load of lime products from Briggs Sidings to Buxton. *Ian Krause*

Right:
One of the most famous views on the ex-Midland Railway Derby–Manchester line through the Peak District is of Monsal Dale Viaduct. In 1966 an unidentified '8F' drifts southwards over the viaduct and crosses the River Wye towards Bakewell with a train of limestone, loaded in iron ore hoppers. *Ian R. Smith*

Right:
The driver of Speke Junction-allocated No 48294 (Beyer Peacock 1941) keeps a close eye on the photographer as his train storms through Bakewell with 8F83, the 2.30pm Kirkby Sidings–Garston load of coal for shipping to Northern Ireland. No 48294 was a resident of Speke Junction from June 1961 to September 1967.
Alan H. Bryant

ICI Hoppers, Buxton–Northwich

Above:
Ex-CLC semaphores predominate as another load of empty hoppers begin their journey back from Northwich to the Peak District on 20 August 1955. Northwich shed has borrowed Longsight's No 48500 (Darlington 1944) for a trip to Tunstead and back. These trains operated up to seven times each day, frequently for an unbroken 365 days each year, for 59 years from 1938 to 1997 (steam-hauled until 1964). Meanwhile, on one of the shed roads, ex-GC 2-8-0 No 63743 of Gorton shed waits to leave the yard. *Brian Morrison*

Left:
Northwich's No 48017 (Crewe 1937) opens up to charge the climb from Altrincham to Hale on 8 June 1964, by which date steam had already been partly displaced on the hoppers by diesels and regular steam haulage had only a few months to run. On the left, in the terminal platforms, one of the original 1931 1,500V DC MSJ&A (Manchester South Junction & Altrincham Railway) electric sets waits to depart for Manchester Oxford Road. This route changed to 25kV AC in 1971 and again to 750V DC in 1991 upon conversion to the Metrolink light-rail system. *N. F. W. Dyckhoff*

Above:
On 7 June 1960 Northwich's No 48605 (Eastleigh 1943) rolls through the former Buxworth station on the down fast line towards New Mills South Junction with 16 loaded hoppers for Northwich. *R. D. Pollard*

Below:
Even after diesels had taken over the workings in 1964, banking the hoppers from Tunstead to Peak Forest Summit was still a steam job. On 26 February 1966 Buxton's No 48748 (Darlington 1946 as LNER 'O6' No 3143) approaches the summit whilst engaged on banking duties. *L. A. Nixon*

Left:
On 10 August 1963 Warrington's No 48557 (Darlington 1945) works a Class 8 Mold Junction–Dewsnap freight into Chester General station. Note that, 40 years after the Grouping, Chester still retains its ex-LNW semaphore signals.
S. D. Wainwright

Below:
Leaving Chester, the North Wales Coast line crosses the River Dee over the Roodee Bridge. On 4 May 1963 Trafford Park's No 48273 (North British 1942), passing Chester racecourse on the right, heads west on the down slow line towards Saltney Junction with the 6.50am Guide Bridge–Mold Junction freight (6D48). The same locomotive features as WD No 560 on page 96. *I. G. Holt*

Above:
On 11 August 1962 Northwich's No 48693 (Brighton 1944) has presumably been borrowed by Crewe South for a trip to Mold Junction and back, being seen hauling a Class 8 freight from Mold Junction to Basford Hall (Crewe) away from Saltney Junction on the up slow line. Behind the locomotive is withdrawn ex-GWR pannier tank No 8734, *en route* from Croes Newydd for scrapping. *Derek Cross*

Right:
The only ex-LNER line in Wales features in this view from November 1964. A recent arrival at Croes Newydd from Willesden, No 48325 (Crewe 1944) climbs the 1-in-45 gradient between Shotton and Buckley with a load of empty 24½-ton mineral wagons from the steelworks at Shotton to Llay Main colliery, reached by a branch line from Caergwrle. *R. Clarke*

Right:
Further west, at Llandudno Junction on 7 September 1961, locally allocated No 48253 (North British 1941) accelerates away towards Colwyn Bay with a Class J load of new ballast from the quarry at Penmaenmawr. The train includes a mixture of Grampus, Catfish and Dogfish ballast wagons on the first stage of their journeys for weekend re-ballasting work. *I. G. Holt*

Right:
The ramparts of Conway Castle tower high above Crewe South's No 48633 (Brighton 1943) as it heads west with the S738 special empty stock for Holyhead on 11 August 1960. In this tranquil scene the goods shed now displays a 'Tunnel Cement Depot' sign, and the coal merchant's lorries are parked up awaiting their next supplies for delivery. *Derek Cross*

Left:
Displaying Class 9 lamps, a local trip begins to descend the steep gradient from Brymbo Middle to Croes Newydd yard at Wrexham in early 1965. Croes Newydd shed had only recently received an allocation of '8Fs', No 48665 (Brighton 1944) being the first of seven '8Fs' to arrive (from November 1964) as replacements for ex-GWR '28xx' 2-8-0s. *A. Wynn*

Left:
A little further south on the ex-GWR main line is Ruabon, junction for Llangollen and Barmouth. Here in 1965 the 7H76 Stanlow–Rowley Regis tank train coasts downhill towards Chirk, hauled by Oxley-allocated No 48475 (Swindon 1945). Even at this date block trains of unfitted tanks were still in use, although being rapidly replaced by more modern vacuum-fitted designs. Note the dual lamp-irons, as fitted to most WR-allocated locomotives. *A. Wynn*

Right:
'Once you're over the viaduct the worst is over' say the engine crews. On 14 April 1961 the Knighton banker is No 48478 (Swindon 1945). With regulator in the roof the locomotive spares no effort assisting the 9.45am Stafford–Pontardulais freight round the stiff 1-in-60 curve through Knucklas Halt, over the viaduct (behind the station nameboard) and on to Llangunllo Summit. The train engine is No 48737 (Darlington 1945 as LNER 'O6' No 3132).
Both locomotives were Shrewsbury residents in 1961. *Ian Allan Library*

Below:
Leaving Llangunllo Tunnel and entering the station, Shrewsbury's No 48369 (Horwich 1944) heads a Class 8 Coton Hill (Shrewsbury)–Llandilo Junction freight on 16 May 1964. With all of the nine miles' hard climbing over, the crew can put their feet up for a well-earned rest.
B. J. Ashworth

Left:
In a scene soon to disappear, the local pick-up goods hauled by Llanelly-allocated No 48328 (Crewe 1944) prepares to drop off wagons at the pretty little station of Penybont, between Knighton and Llandrindod Wells, on 5 June 1964. The section on to Llandrindod remained as double-track-only until the rationalisation and passenger dieselisation of the Central Wales line began 10 days later. From 10 August through freights were diverted away over the North & West route via Hereford. *Derek Cross*

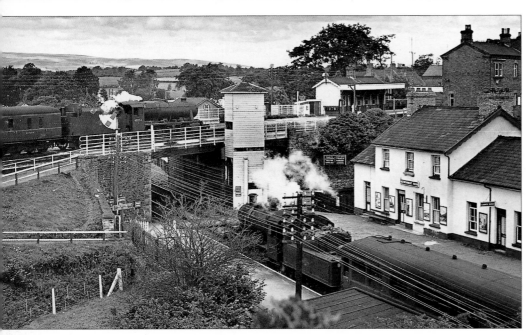

Left:
Passenger trains meet at Builth Road station on 29 August 1962. At the High Level platforms Shrewsbury's No 48354 (Horwich 1944) runs in with the 12.20pm Swansea Victoria–Shrewsbury service as Moat Lane's Ivatt Class 2 2-6-0 No 46516 waits at the Low Level platform with the 1.20pm Brecon–Moat Lane train. The station boasted full facilities, including a refreshment room, lifts and ramped access between High and Low Level platforms. The Low Level platforms were to close with the Mid-Wales line on 31 December 1962. *B. J. Ashworth*

Lower left:
On 29 August 1962 a pair of Llanelly-based '8Fs', Nos 48409 (Swindon 1943) and 48524 (Doncaster 1944), accelerate away from Builth Road and cross the River Wye with a southbound freight. *B. J. Ashworth*

Right:
The other section of the Central Wales line on which freight trains required banking was that northbound between Llandovery and Sugar Loaf Summit. On 24 March 1961 the guard gives a friendly wave to the banking locomotive as Llanelly's No 48172 (Crewe 1943) prepares to drop off the train at Sugar Loaf loop and return light engine to Llandovery, ready to assist the next northbound freight. *Anthony A. Vickers*

Above:
Viewed from above the tunnel a northbound freight, headed by one '8F' and banked by another, storms up the last few yards of the seven-mile climb from Llandovery to Sugar Loaf Summit on 30 October 1961. Banking survived to 10 August 1964, whereafter through freights were diverted away. *B. J. Ashworth*

Right:
On 27 July 1962 Standard 2-6-4T No 80097, a recent arrival at Swansea's East Dock shed from the newly electrified London, Tilbury & Southend (LTS) line, departs from Pontardulais station with the 5.35pm Swansea Victoria–Llandebie local passenger train. Waiting to follow from the Llanelly line is Llanelly's No 48434 (Swindon 1944) with a Class 7 Llandilo Junction–Shrewsbury freight. When the ex-LNW Paxton Street shed in Swansea closed in August 1959 the provision of passenger motive power passed first to Landore and later to East Dock, when the Wind Street Viaduct was weight-restricted in 1963.
Leslie Sandler

Right:
By the spring of 1964 there were very few surviving steam workings on the South Wales main line. At the west end of Cardiff General station on 25 May Llanelly's No 48760 (Doncaster 1945 as LNER 'O6' No 3155) coasts through with a Class 7 Llandilo Junction–Rood End (Langley Green) block load of steel billets on Bogie Bolster E wagons. This was a long-standing flow of special steels, which ceased only when the Llanelly steelworks closed in 1968.
S. Rickard / J&J Collection

Right:
On 19 August 1964 Barrs Court Junction signalbox at Hereford has routed Shrewsbury's No 48404 (Swindon 1943) and its Class 8 pick-up goods from Shrewsbury onto the freight avoiding line to Barton rather than towards Barrs Court and the passenger station. This was the original route through Hereford, which became freight-only when the separate route through Barrs Court passenger station was constructed. Note that both of the distant signals are 'fixed' as an economy measure.
B. J. Ashworth

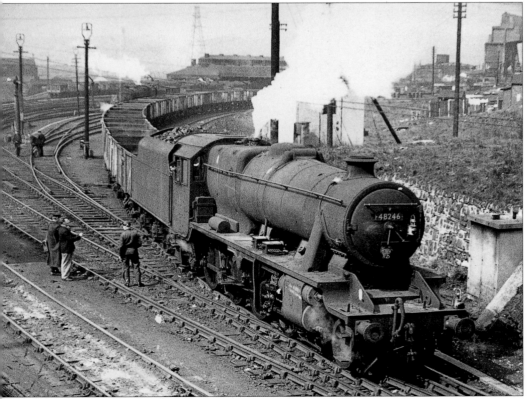

Above:
Alsager, located between Crewe and Kidsgrove, was a busy area serving several collieries. In this view from 1962 Toton's No 48685 (Brighton 1944), running under clear signals, storms by with a Class J load of coal empties from Dundas Sidings (Sandycroft, west of Chester) to Pratts Sidings at Stoke. *J. Winkle*

Left:
On 22 April 1965 at Pratts Sidings (Stoke) locally allocated No 48246 (North British 1940) draws empty coal wagons forward ready to supply local collieries via Hem Heath sidings. In the right background is the coaling plant at Stoke shed. Pratts later became known as Cockshute Sidings. *P. Dorney*

Right:
Priestfield Junction, just south of Wolverhampton, is where the original Oxford, Worcester & Wolverhampton (OWW) line via Dudley joined the later direct line from Birmingham Snow Hill to Wolverhampton. The lines on the right served an Esso oil depot, whilst those on the left climbed up the bank to connect with Walsall Street freight depot (now Wolverhampton Steel Terminal). On 4 June 1962 Heaton Mersey's No 48429 (Swindon 1944) carries Class J headlamps with an unidentified block load of sheeted minerals, heading south towards Bilston and Wednesbury. *Brian Moone/Kidderminster Railway Museum*

Left:
At Coseley Deepfields, on the Stour Valley line between Wolverhampton and Tipton, the down main is relaid with new bullhead rail on 13 March 1955. Engaged in moving materials are Bescot's No 48767 (Doncaster 1946 as LNER 'O6' No 3162) on the down line and Crewe South-allocated No 48294 (Beyer Peacock 1941) on the up. Spectators watch permanent-way staff tighten fishplates as a classic Midland Red single-deck bus crosses the overbridge at Coseley station. *Michael Hale*

Right:
The Prince's End branch, between Wednesbury and Tipton, lost its passenger service as early as 1916 but survived as a useful freight route until April 1981. Viewed from a window at Ocker Hill power station in July 1965, Wellingborough-allocated No 48082 (Vulcan Foundry 1937) brings loaded iron-ore hoppers from the East Midlands (via Walsall and the Prince's End branch) to the steelworks at Spring Vale between Coseley and Wolverhampton. In the background Bogie Bolsters await unloading in the bottom yard of Wednesbury Steel Terminal. *W. J. A. Haskins*

Upper left:
At Pleck Junction the tracks west of Walsall divide into Wolverhampton, Dudley and Bescot routes.
On 21 August 1964 a mixed freight heads west onto the Dudley line, hauled by Bescot's No 48522 (Doncaster 1944). On the right are the carriage sidings at Midland Yard, while at work in the background (left) is the Pleck Gasworks 0-4-0 Peckett shunter. *Peter Fitton*

Lower left:
Bescot-allocated No 48175 (Crewe 1943) blows off impatiently as it is checked at Perry Barr station on the Aston–Bushbury (the original Grand Junction) line with a Class J freight for Bescot Yard on 26 June 1957. Property redevelopment and railway electrification have since made this scene unrecognisable. *Michael Mensing*

Upper right:
On 31 October 1964 Heaton Mersey-allocated No 48191 (North British 1942) approaches Penns station (on the Sutton Park line) on its way towards Walsall and Stourbridge with a Class 8 load of sugar beet for the factory at Kidderminster.
Michael Mensing

Centre right:
With Water Orton yard in the background, Burton-allocated No 48000 (Crewe 1935), running tender-first but still carrying Class 1 headlamps, attempts to regain some lost time as it heads for Birmingham New Street with the 1V70 Newcastle–Swansea express on 8 July 1963. The '8F' had come to the rescue at Kingsbury branch sidings when 'Peak' Type 4 diesel No D40 was declared a failure. *Vic Smith*

Lower right:
The line from Nuneaton to Arley Tunnel climbs at a gradient of 1 in 126. On 11 December 1965 a Class 9 load of coal from Newdigate Colliery (on the Coventry–Nuneaton line) to Hams Hall power station has '8F' superpower as Nuneaton's No 48650 (Eastleigh 1943) storms through Stockingford, assisted by another unidentified '8F'.
J. H. Cooper-Smith

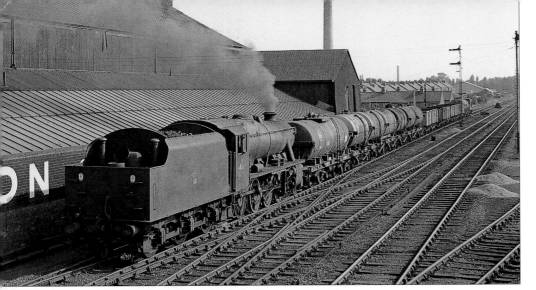

Left:
Foleshill, in the northern suburbs of Coventry on the line to Nuneaton, was the terminus of the Foleshill Light Railway, which served an industrial complex around the Courtaulds factory. On 24 June 1961 Nuneaton's No 48686 (Brighton 1944) hauls a Class J freight onto the Light Railway with a mixed load of ICI tanks and coal. The Light Railway closed on 8 April 1972. *Michael Mensing*

Left:
Kingswinford South Junction is where the freight line from the Pensnett Trading Estate and Oxley joined the OWW route between Dudley and Stourbridge. On 28 April 1956 Bescot's No 48762 (Doncaster 1946 as LNER 'O6' No 3157) brings a long Class H load of Cannock Chase mined coal for Stourport-on-Severn power station downhill towards Stourbridge Junction. The train will have required banking assistance up the steep climb from Great Bridge to Dudley. The site of the yard on the left, then known as Brettell Lane, is now occupied by Brierley Hill Steel Terminal. *Michael Hale*

Lower left:
Its 10 non-corridor coaches apparently well filled, a Bank Holiday Monday excursion (1X49) from Walsall to Stourport rolls through Kidderminster towards Hartlebury on 1 August 1960. Stourport, on the banks of the River Severn, was a popular day-trip destination for both holidaymakers and fishermen. As banking engines are not normally available on a Bank Holiday Toton-allocated No 48661 (Eastleigh 1944) has been borrowed for the job, presumably because of its ability to climb the bank to Dudley without assistance. The locomotive is passing a GWR shunter's truck and a locally based Toad brake van. The goods yard in the background (left) is now the site of the Severn Valley Railway's Kidderminster Town station, while the goods shed is occupied by the SVR's carriage works.
Brian Moone/Kidderminster Railway Museum

Right:
Warwick's No 48531 (Doncaster 1945) rolls past Bewdley North signalbox on 29 June 1966 with a load of coal from Alveley Colliery, on the Severn Valley line, to Stourport power station. This scene has changed little in the intervening four decades, the most visible alteration being the replacement of the modern-style electric platform lights with more traditional gas-style lighting.
Roger Siviter

Above:
On Saturday 27 April 1963 Villa Park hosted an FA Cup semi-final match between Southampton and Manchester United. Southampton supporters were brought to Birmingham on a total of 13 specials, some of which were routed from Oxford via Worcester and Stourbridge, their respective Bulleid Pacifics being piloted up Old Hill Bank from Stourbridge Junction by '8Fs'. Here Stourbridge's No 48417 (Swindon 1943) draws into Snow Hill piloting rebuilt 'West Country' No 34039 *Boscastle* with one of the specials. On the up goods line the crew of a 'Large Prairie' tank watch the spectacle as they wait for the road with their local trip freight to Bordesley yard. On the down goods unrebuilt 'West Country' No 34094 *Mortehoe*, having arrived with an earlier special via Leamington, waits to visit Tyseley depot for servicing, the empty stock having been taken forward to Worcester for cleaning and stabling. Another 'West Country'+'8F' combination observed was of Nos 48478 and 34009 *Lyme Regis*.
A. W. V. Mace/Kidderminster Railway Museum

Left:
The lampman is at work on the signal gantry at Bromsgrove North in July 1961 as Toton's No 48350 (Horwich 1944) begins to move forward with a Class H freight for Washwood Heath (Birmingham). In the distance can be seen the smoke from the banker ('9F' No 92079) as it takes up the strain of pushing the train up the 1-in-36 Lickey Incline to Blackwell.
J. Davenport

Left:
At Bromsgrove South on 16 June 1966 water cascades from the overflowing tender of Saltley's No 48336 (Horwich 1943) as, refreshed after descending the Lickey Incline and with a full head of steam, the locomotive prepares to resume its progress westward with a Class 8 coal train for Gloucester.
Anthony A. Vickers

Left:
South of Lapworth, on the GW main line to Leamington, Tyseley's No 48035 (Vulcan Foundry 1936) hauls a short Class 3 freight of five Carflats, carrying new Minis and Land Rovers from Dorridge to Southampton Docks on 20 September 1966.
Michael Mensing

Left:
On 14 October 1964 Kirkby-in-Ashfield's No 48225 (North British 1942) coasts through Hatton with a Class 7 coal train for Banbury. The line to the left is the branch to Bearley and Stratford-upon-Avon. Note that the LMR has changed some signals to upper quadrants since acquiring this ex-GW route; also the GW ATC ramp in the 'four-foot' of the down main line. *J. S. Hancock*

Right:
Cropredy station (closed 1956) served passengers on the line from Banbury to Leamington. On 12 March 1966, half a mile north of the site of the former station, Mold Junction's No 48458 (Swindon 1944) is climbing as it transfers a load of chalk loaded in iron-ore hoppers from Ardley to the cement works at Harbury. *Michael Mensing*

Right:
Ettington station was located on the last surviving section of the former SMJ (Stratford-upon-Avon & Midland Junction) line between Fenny Compton and Stratford Racecourse. Between 1960 and final closure on 1 March 1965 the line enjoyed a new lease of life, a chord at Stratford allowing its use as a diversionary route for iron-ore trains between Banbury and South Wales, thereby avoiding the climb of Hatton Bank and shortening the journey by more than 20 miles. On the last working day (27 February 1965) Tyseley's No 48474 (Swindon 1945) makes steady progress through the switched-out loop with a Banbury–Llanwern Class 8 load of ore in tipplers. *Ron Fisher*

Above:
Neath-allocated No 48760 (Doncaster 1945 as LNER 'O6' No 3155) makes light of the five-mile climb at 1 in 100 up Campden Bank with a Severn Tunnel Junction–Oxford Class 8 coal train on 28 September 1964. The train will have reversed at Honeybourne, where the banker will have been attached to assist as far as Moreton-in-Marsh. *F. A. Haynes*

Left:
Lansdown Junction, just south of Cheltenham, was where the Midland and GW Birmingham–Bristol lines met, the two thereafter running parallel as far as Gloucester. In this view Tyseley's No 48474 (Swindon 1945) heads west with a Class 8 Washwood Heath (Birmingham)–Stoke Gifford (Bristol) service on 20 May 1964. The train has taken the Stratford route, preferred for slower freights because of its easier gradients and lighter traffic levels. The two wagons behind the locomotive are Trestrols, special vehicles designed for carrying large steel plates which would otherwise be 'out-of-gauge'. *W. G. Sumner*

Above:
Another load of iron-ore empties leaves Gloucester Central station and approaches Tramway Junction on 27 April 1965, returning to Banbury from Severn Tunnel Junction. Oxley-allocated No 48738 (Darlington 1945 as LNER 'O6' No 3133) appears to have been borrowed on the basis that Banbury will find work hauling ore to Spring Vale to get the locomotive home — or had Banbury borrowed it for a trip to South Wales and back? The lines to the left are the ex-Midland route to Bristol via Gloucester Eastgate station. On the right a 'Hall' and 'Black Five' are stabled on Gloucester shed. *Derek Cross*

Right:
Grange Court Junction, where the Hereford–Gloucester and Severn Tunnel Junction–Gloucester lines met, was located a few miles west of Gloucester. Seen in July 1964, Willesden-allocated No 48134 (Crewe 1941) is far from home as it hauls an eastbound block load of sheeted 16-ton mineral wagons conveying basic slag fertiliser from a South Wales steelworks to the Midlands. In 1956 this locomotive had acquired tender No 9003; originally allocated to No 46202 *Princess Anne* (the 'Turbomotive'), this was an early curve-sided Stanier-type tender (coal capacity 9 tons, water 4,000 gallons) fitted with roller bearings. *P. Cookson*

Above:
In the autumn of 1948 the newly nationalised railways decided to conduct Locomotive Exchanges between the locomotives of the former 'Big Four' prior to any decision on new designs. The exchanges were conducted 'home' and 'away' in the three categories — 'express passenger', 'mixed traffic' and 'freight'. The five freight types selected for testing were ex-GW '28xx' 2-8-0, ex-LMS '8F' 2-8-0, ex-LNER 'O1' 2-8-0 and ex-WD 2-8-0 and 2-10-0. Locomotives on 'away' territory were worked by 'home' crews familiar with the type, who then spent time familiarising themselves with the 'foreign' routes involved. The tests involved use of dynamometer cars in order to assess work done and fuel consumption. Little direction seems to have been given to the crews, so that wide variations in handling were displayed, rendering results largely inconclusive. The '8Fs' acquitted themselves very well and proved almost as economical as the '28xx', which had the advantage of working only on 'home' territory with Welsh coal because of route-availability problems off the former GWR. One of the four routes used was Severn Tunnel Junction–Acton; here we see one of the test trains, complete with dynamometer car, climbing away from the Severn Tunnel through Patchway behind Sheffield Grimesthorpe-based No 48189 (North British 1942). Running with a tender in LMS livery, this locomotive was selected as being of average mileage and condition, replacing Swindon-built No 48400 which was found to be rather run-down. No 48189 had received a General overhaul at Crewe in October 1947 and following selection received an unclassified inspection, again at Crewe, in June 1948. *R. J. Leonard / Kidderminster Railway Museum*

Left:
Hawkeridge Junction lies just to the north of Westbury, on the Bath–Salisbury line. On 13 February 1965 Birkenhead's No 48684 (Brighton 1944) coasts through towards Westbury with a Class 7 load of empty petrol tanks from Bromford Bridge to Fawley via Salisbury. Note the barrier wagons at each end of the train, required because of the flammable nature of the load. On the right is the Westbury-avoiding line to Westbury East Loop, Heywood Road Junction and Reading. *Ivo Peters*

Above:
No 48436 (Swindon 1944) of St Philip's Marsh (Bristol) rolls past the north end of the Weston-super-Mare-avoiding line at Worle Junction with a Class E Burton–Tavistock Junction (Plymouth) express freight on 30 July 1961. Note the WR-style vacuum ejector, needed to create the WR's standard 25in of vacuum. *Michael J. Fox*

Right:
Teignmouth's beach seems very quiet for 1 July 1957 as St Philip's Marsh-allocated No 48475 (Swindon 1945) heads east along the sea wall towards Dawlish with a long Class E express freight from Tavistock Junction to Stoke Gifford. *R. C. Riley*

Left:
At Nuneaton Trent Valley station in March 1959 the driver of locally allocated No 48111 (Crewe 1939) looks back for the shunter's hand signal as he makes up his train in the up yard. Behind, in the up slow platform, 'Jubilee' No 45731 *Perseverance* blows off impatiently while waiting to depart for Euston with a parcels train. The new Platforms 6 and 7, constructed recently on the site of the up sidings, now fill the view at this location.
Horace H. Bleads

West Coast Main Line
Nuneaton–Euston

Below:
The young fireman looks a little bored as Crewe South-allocated No 48287 (Beyer Peacock 1940) coasts off Newbold water troughs and slows for Rugby with a Class H up mixed freight on 29 April 1958. The crew have decided not to bother taking water, as there will be plenty of time for the relief crew to 'put the bag in' whilst the train stands at Rugby. Note the 'X' sign alongside the down fast line, indicating the start of the water troughs.
Michael Mensing

Above:
The overhead is already erected but not yet energised at Ashton, south of Roade, on 11 March 1964 as Wellingborough's No 48609 (Eastleigh 1943) roars by with a long rake of empty non-corridor stock.
K. C. H. Fairey / Robin Cullup collection

Centre right:
By August Bank Holiday (3 August) 1964 electrification at Bletchley had not yet proceeded as far as erection of the overhead wires. Curious passengers throng the down fast platform as a dead English Electric Type 4 (Class 40) diesel, which had failed in the Leighton Buzzard area with the morning Euston–Blackpool service, is rescued by Northampton's No 48440 (Swindon 1944).
I. J. Hodson

Lower right:
North of Watford Junction the fast and slow lines through the Watford Tunnels run on slightly separated alignments. Having emerged on the up slow line on 9 August 1952, Willesden-allocated No 48632 (Brighton 1943) coasts south with a Class J train of mostly sheeted mineral wagons for Willesden.
Brian Morrison

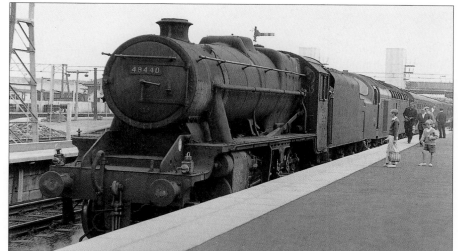

Above:

Two '8Fs' meet on Bushey troughs, south of Watford, in 1960. Southbound Toton-allocated No 48490 (Horwich 1945) passes Bescot's Fowler-tendered No 48733 (Darlington 1945 as LNER 'O6' No 3128) heading north with a Class D express freight. Note in the foreground the 'DC line' used by both BR and Underground trains to Watford, hence the provision of third and fourth rails. *Robin Cullup collection*

Left:

On 25 March 1953 at Bushey No 48626 (Brighton 1943) heads for home at Willesden with a Class J mixed freight. The large tank behind the train is the water-softening plant for the water troughs, located behind the photographer. *Brian Morrison*

Left:

A Class H block load of coal from Toton to Willesden coasts through Hatch End on 26 April 1962, hauled by Cricklewood-allocated No 48770 (Doncaster 1946 as LNER 'O6' No 3165). The first five wagons are some of the ex-LMS 1929-built 40-ton bogie hoppers designed to supply coal to the ex-LNWR Stonebridge Park power station which, until its closure in 1967, provided power for the Euston–Watford 'DC' line. *Peter E. Baughan*

Right:
Before rebuilding of the station under a concrete raft rendered the location hardly recognisable, Willesden-allocated No 48368 (Horwich 1944) brings a Class 8 mixed freight through the old Wembley Central on the up fast line in May 1963. The headlamps display the dedicated cross-London code for Willesden–Hither Green, although this load appears to have started further north, possibly at Watford. The locomotive acquired its Fowler tender in a special visit to Crewe in April 1960 and regained a Stanier tender (ex No 48262) in December 1965. *Derek Rhodda*

Right:
With the new power 'box visible in the background, electrification work looks complete as Bescot's No 48674 (Ashford 1944) backs a Class 9 load of old track panels past Willesden locomotive shed *en route* to South West Sidings on 8 August 1965. The train is 'topped-and-tailed', being headed by another '8F'. The site of Willesden shed was later occupied by a Freightliner terminal, while the power 'box has only recently been replaced. *R. C. Riley*

Right:
Willesden's No 48122 (Crewe 1939) waits to depart Euston's Platform 3 with the empty stock from the incoming 'Mancunian' on 3 August 1958. On the right, departing for Watford, is one of the soon-to-be-replaced ex-LNWR electric sets. *Brian Morrison*

The East Midlands

Above:
Tapton Junction, to the north of Chesterfield, is where the original North Midland line to Rotherham and the North separates from the later Sheffield loop line. With Tapton Junction's tall semaphores visible just ahead of the road bridge in the distance, Derby's No 48005 (Crewe 1935) heads towards Chesterfield on the up fast line with a lengthy Class H mixed freight in the late 1950s; note the engineer's crane and supporting van leading. On the left a Midland Class 3F 0-6-0 shunts the sidings. Subsequently this area became a scrapyard dismantling large numbers of steam locomotives. *T. G. Hepburn*

Left:
At Pye Bridge, on the Erewash Valley line, Wellingborough's No 48061 (Vulcan Foundry 1936) heads for home with a Class F train of empty iron-ore tipplers on the up main line in the early 1960s. Note the typical Midland-style fencing (at the back of the down main platform), the gas lighting and typical Erewash scenery. *Robin Cullup collection*

Right:
To the south of Pye Bridge lies Codnor Park, where on Saturday 8 May 1965 Westhouses-allocated No 48046 (Vulcan Foundry 1936) was heading south with a Class 7 load of iron-ore empties for the mines of Northamptonshire.
M. York

Below:
Seen departing Mansfield Town station on 6 August 1961, Kettering's No 48645 (Brighton 1943) has been borrowed by Mansfield and carries Class A headlamps to work a short (half-day) excursion to Matlock. This will be routed via Pye Bridge and Ambergate, traversing the section now occupied by the preserved Midland Railway Centre line. Mansfield Town station closed on 12 October 1964 but reopened as part of the 'Robin Hood' line on 20 November 1995.
J. Cupit

Left:
Disaster at Kirkby-in-Ashfield shed (16B) in April 1959, locally allocated No 48193 (North British 1942) having run out of one of the stabling roads and into the turntable pit. The breakdown gang and higher authority discuss tactics as the hydraulic 'Kelbus' gear slowly raises the locomotive back onto an even keel. The locomotive will then be drawn slowly back onto the rails. Following recovery No 48193 visited Derby Works in May for an unclassified checkover. *F. Ashley*

Below:
On 31 July 1958 Crewe South-allocated No 48248 (North British 1940), heading a Class J Colwick–Stanlow train of empty tank wagons, emerges from Mapperley Tunnel on the ex-GN Nottingham-avoiding line via Gedling. The train will be routed via the Bagthorpe junctions, Derby Friargate, Egginton Junction, Stoke, Lawton Junction, Sandbach, Middlewich and Mouldsworth. Following an earlier collapse (in 1925) which had closed the line for several months, Mapperley Tunnel was finally declared unsafe in January 1959, trains being diverted via Nottingham Victoria. *T. Boustead*

Right:
The 3.15am Class E Willesden Brent–Colwick express freight followed an interesting route reflecting the pre-Grouping running powers of the LNWR over the GN Grantham–Nottingham line: from Northampton the train was routed via Market Harborough, John O'Gaunt and Saxondale Junction. On the misty grey early morning of Friday 21 July 1961 the train rushes north at about 50mph just west of Saxondale Junction, near journey's end. Nottingham's No 48377 (Horwich 1944) has responsibility for the load of 26 wagons and brake. *M. C. Neale / Robin Cullup collection*

Left:
On 18 March 1964 Kirkby's No 48395 (Horwich 1945) coasts past an adverse distant signal at Beeston South Junction with a long Class 7 load of empty 24½- ton coal hoppers from Drakelow power station to Calverton Colliery. *K. Bale*

Below:
With the large Beeston sleeper depot in the background, Nottingham's No 48117 (Crewe 1939) pulls a Class J load of coal for Toton out of the goods loop and on to the up main in 1954. The numerous tank wagons in the sleeper depot contain creosote for treating wooden sleepers. For many years the depot was home to 1936-built Fowler 0-4-0 diesel shunters ED5 and ED10. *Peter Wayman*

Left:
In 1961 Kirkby-allocated No 48272 (North British 1942) blackens the sky over Trent Station North Junction with a Class J train of at least 70 loaded 16-ton mineral wagons destined for Castle Donington power station. The line to the right, overlooked by a terrace of railway cottages, leads to Beeston and Nottingham. The cottages survive to this day, with Trent power 'box now located alongside. *A. W. Smith*

Right:
The joint nature of the former GN/LNW line north of Melton Mowbray is revealed by the clear GNR design of the signalbox at Scalford. Northampton-allocated No 48360 (Horwich 1944) has run round its train and is preparing to take empty iron-ore hoppers up the branch to the mines at Eaton on 4 April 1959. When loaded the hoppers will return to Corby via Market Harborough and Kettering. The branch closed the following month, the main line in September 1964. *Hugh Davies / Robin Cullup collection*

Left:
Coalville, at the centre of the busy North West Leicestershire Coalfield, for many years had a large allocation of '8Fs'. Stabled in steam on their home shed on 26 July 1965 are Nos 48137 (Crewe 1941), 48699 (Brighton 1944) and 48617 (Brighton 1943). The shed (15E) closed in April 1966. *Ivo Peters*

Above:

Oakham Level Crossing signalbox achieved fame following its selection as the prototype for the Airfix '00'-gauge kit, which retailed for 2s (10p!) in the early 1960s. In 1959 Kettering's No 48124 (Crewe 1939), with young fireman Bryan Benford leaning from the cab, works through Oakham with a Class F train of empty mineral wagons destined probably for the ironstone quarries at Storefield or Cranford. If a shortage of tipplers caused steel-bodied 16-ton mineral wagons to be used for ironstone traffic the side and end doors would be welded up, temporarily converting them to tipplers. Did the little boy in the pram ever grow up to be an engine driver? *N. E. Stead / Robin Cullup collection*

Right:

On 22 June 1960 Willesden's No 48603 (Eastleigh 1943) heads west away from Peterborough East with a Class H mixed freight from Whitemoor to Rugby. The Fowler tender had been acquired during a visit to Crewe Works in December 1958. Visible in the background is the coaling tower at Peterborough Spital shed. The train will soon pass through Wansford over what is now the preserved Nene Valley Railway.
D. C. Ovenden

Right:
On 18 May 1964 Wellingborough-allocated No 48374 (Horwich 1944) coasts to a stop at Glendon sidings, ready to back in with its Class 8 load of empty iron-ore tipplers. The sidings are just north of Glendon South Junction, where the Corby and Manton line separates from the Midland main line, just north of Kettering. The ironstone workings at Glendon opened in 1863 and closed with the end of steel-making at Corby in 1981. As late as the 1970s some 10,000 tons per week was being despatched to Corby. *R. C. Riley*

Left:
On the afternoon of 20 February 1964 Wellingborough's No 48082 (Vulcan Foundry 1937) heads east on the Rugby–Market Harborough line through Lilbourne with a Class 5 express freight from Rugby to Whitemoor (March). The first three vehicles are cattle wagons carrying Irish store cattle from Holyhead to Spalding for market, having been detached at Rugby from the Holyhead–Broad Street fast freight. The line via Lilbourne closed in June 1966 in favour of the longer route via Leicester. *Peter E. Baughan*

Left:
Stretching the East Midlands. The 1962/3 'Big Freeze' has clearly already begun as Bletchley's No 48668 (Brighton 1944) runs through Sandy with the lightly loaded 10.8am Class 9 branch freight from Bletchley to Cambridge on 29 December 1962. *Kidderminster Railway Museum*

Midland Main Line, Leicester–St Pancras

Above:
On 30 September 1959 Coalville-allocated No 48644 (Brighton 1943) has a clear road as it accelerates a northbound Class H load of assorted empty ironstone hoppers off the Coalville branch at Knighton North Junction and towards Knighton Tunnel and Leicester. The train is probably heading for the ironstone mines at Cottesmore. *G. D. King*

Right:
Desborough & Rothwell station closed on 1 January 1968. On 30 May 1959, however, closure is in nobody's thoughts as Toton's No 48195 (North British 1942), having breasted the five-mile climb at 1-in-132 from Market Harborough, coasts downhill through the neat and tidy platforms with a Class J mineral train (including concrete pipes loaded in two tube wagons). *R. C. Riley*

Above:
In April 1960 these beautiful ex-Midland wooden-arm-and-post lower-quadrant signals at Kettering South still had a further two years to survive before resignalling swept them away. Here Northampton's No 48422 (Swindon 1943) coasts past with the Class H 3.10pm Wellingborough–Chaddesden (Derby) freight. Much of the load appears to consist of 'green card' defective wagons, destined for grading at Chaddesden sidings before allocation to workshops for repair. *R. F. Collins / Robin Cullup collection*

Left:
At Burton Latimer, the home of 'Weetabix', Toton-allocated No 48182 (North British 1942) rolls past the abandoned platforms on the up goods line with a Toton–Wellingborough Class J load of domestic coal in 1959. Burton Latimer station, the first south of Kettering, had closed on 20 November 1950.
R. F. Collins / Robin Cullup collection

Above:
Despite Nationalisation in January 1948, Wellingborough's No 48692 (Brighton 1944) emerged from a General overhaul at Crewe in September 1948 still displaying 'L M S' on its tender. Here, in the early spring of 1949, the locomotive heads a Class J load of coal from Toton through Harper Lane Cutting, between Napsbury and Radlett. The large painted 'X' on the cabside signifies this locomotive's participation in a 1946 water-treatment experiment involving 50 '8Fs' restricted to work between Toton and Cricklewood. *Ian Allan Library*

Right:
Up and down freights meet on 21 March 1953 as Wellingborough's No 48150 (Crewe 1942) emerges from Elstree Tunnel with a Class F express freight and passes classmate from Kettering No 48143 (Crewe 1942) heading for Cricklewood. *Brian Morrison*

The Great Central

Left:
Between Nottingham Victoria and New Basford stations lies Sherwood Rise Tunnel, where at 6.56pm on Monday 29 July 1963 Annesley's No 48304 (Crewe 1943) was photographed heading north with a load of empty 16-ton mineral wagons *en route* from Woodford Halse to Annesley. *T. Boustead*

Below left:
On 16 May 1964 locally allocated No 48088 (Vulcan Foundry 1937) leaves Woodford Halse for Culworth and the South with a short (10-wagon) Class 6 oil train. *Ivo Peters*

Right:
The down platform at Leicester Central station is deserted apart from a member of the locomotive crew as No 48287 (Beyer Peacock 1940) calls with the 6.30am Banbury–Nottingham Victoria Class 3 parcels train on 11 June 1966.
The locomotive is far from home, being allocated to Croes Newydd shed (6C) at Wrexham. *M. Mitchell*

Below:
The chord linking the ex-Midland Acton Wells–Cricklewood line with the GC line at Neasden Junction is traversed on 6 September 1963 by Aston-allocated No 48719 (Brighton 1944 for LNER as 'O6' No 7665). The locomotive is descending to the GC with a Class 9 trip carrying long reinforcing steel rods on Bogie Bolster D wagons. The lines in the foreground had led to the former Neasden GC locomotive shed; following track-lifting the area soon became a coal yard. Note in the background (left) the Underground station at Neasden, complete with Bakerloo Line tube train. *Peter Groom*

Left:
Bletchley-allocated No 48207 (North British 1942) brings a seemingly endless load of Hinksey–Swanbourne coal empties across Wolvercot Junction onto the Bletchley line, north of Oxford, in the early 1960s. In the distance (right) is the coal stage at Oxford shed (81F). *J. A. Coiley*

Below:
On 14 September 1963 Woodford Halse-allocated No 48005 (Crewe 1935) brings a Woodford–Reading Class 8 mixed freight through Oxford station. The eight empty cattle wagons behind the locomotive will have been attached at Banbury for return to Fishguard. *Robin Cullup collection*

Right:
In August 1964 north- and southbound freights pass on the main lines at High Wycombe. Woodford Halse's No 48387 (Horwich 1945), hauling a northbound Class 7 train of empty mineral wagons, meets Tyseley-allocated No 6879 *Overton Grange* heading south for Acton. *Ian Krause*

Below:
No 48387 was also in action on Tuesday 30 July 1963, being borrowed from an up freight as a replacement for a 'Western' diesel-hydraulic which had failed at Princes Risborough with the 7.10am Shrewsbury–Paddington express. Here the '8F' brings the train triumphantly past Westbourne Park and into Paddington. *George Staddon / N. Stead collection*

Left:
Kensington Olympia station was the usual point for locomotive changeovers on inter-regional trains to/from the Southern Region. On 6 August 1960 the 10-coach 12.32pm Hastings–Manchester London Road (soon to be renamed Piccadilly) holiday extra, having arrived behind BR Class 4 4-6-0 No 75075, departs behind Holbeck's No 48158 (Crewe 1943). Blowing off vigorously ready for the road, this 'starred 8' (similar to No 48680 described on page 42) would be well capable of running at speeds of up to 70mph on the West Coast main line, which would be busy with holiday trains on this summer Saturday. The locomotive had yet to receive AWS equipment, eventually fitted during a special visit to Horwich in October 1960. *R. C. Riley*

Left:
Cricklewood-allocated No 48132 (Crewe 1941) heads a Hither Green–Brent Sidings (Cricklewood) freight through Clapham Junction (Reading side) in 1958. The headlamps display the correct code for a train from Hither Green to Brent via Nunhead, Factory Junction and Barnes. Note the 'M7' tank on Waterloo empty stock in the carriage sidings on the right. *Peter Treloar*

Left:
On the Brighton side at Clapham Junction, having passed over the West London line, Toton-allocated No 48672 (Ashford 1944) displays the headlamp code for Willesden, Clapham and Norwood Junction with a cross-London freight on 16 March 1964. *R. L. Sewell*

Right:
On the last day of regular services at Bath Green Park station, Saturday 5 March 1966, locally allocated No 48760 (Doncaster 1945 as LNER 'O6' No 3155) shunts the empty stock for the 8.15am local passenger train to Templecombe. *Derek Cross*

Below:
More usual work for No 48760 is demonstrated here on the approach to Devonshire Tunnel as it takes the last load of S&D-route empty minerals from Bath to Writhlington Colliery, near Radstock, on 4 March 1966. *Michael J. Fox*

The Somerset & Dorset

Above:
On a frosty 15 January 1963 the Mendips had been covered with a blanketing of snow for more than two weeks as Bath-allocated No 48737 (Darlington 1945 as LNER 'O6' No 3132) passes Midford with the 6.25am goods from Evercreech Junction to Bath. The locomotive is mounting a vigorous assault on the climb to Combe Down, but the fireman has apparently misjudged his boiler-water level, causing 'priming' (corrected by the driver opening the cylinder draincocks). *Ivo Peters*

Left:
Weather conditions at Midford are much more pleasant on 3 May 1961 as No 48450 (Swindon 1944) works a northbound test freight. The '8F' was on loan from St Philip's Marsh with a view to replacing the ex-S&D 2-8-0s, by now reaching the end of their working lives. For working over the S&D route No 48450 had been specially fitted at Bath with tablet-catching apparatus, visible here extended from the tender front after being used to collect the tablet at Midford signalbox for the single-line section onwards to Bath. *Ivo Peters*

Right:
On 17 August 1963 Bath's No 48737 blows off hard as it coasts onto the double-line section at Midford with train 1X04, a nine-van pigeon special from the Midlands to Templecombe. Pigeon specials were once big business for the railway: homing clubs would charter a whole train from which railway staff would simultaneously liberate the birds for a race home.
Ivo Peters

Left:
A fresh fall of snow on the Mendip Hills has required snow-clearance operations on 6 January 1963. Plough-fitted 'Jinty' No 47496 is assisted in this task by '8F' No 48660 (Eastleigh 1943), the pair having just cleared the line between Binegar and Midsomer Norton. Both locomotives were allocated to Bath Green Park.
Ivo Peters

Right:
Pictured in the sylvan setting of Parkstone Bank, between Branksome and Poole, Bath-allocated No 48470 (Swindon 1945) returns north with the 1.10pm local from Bournemouth West to Bath on 3 August 1964. Earlier in the day No 48470 worked into Bournemouth with the 9.5am local from Templecombe. Note the tablet-catching apparatus on the tender's leading edge. *Ivo Peters*

Above:
Wartime photos of '8Fs' in WD condition are understandably very rare. Here, on 7 May 1943, WD No 560 (North British 1942) heads north through Sileby (north of Leicester) with a train of empty coke wagons. No 560 was delivered as part of the final Ministry of Supply order, but not all locomotives could be sent overseas immediately, No 560 being initially loaned to the LMS. The intended move to Iran was then cancelled, whereupon the locomotive was transferred to LMS stock, becoming No 8273 in December 1943. Note the close similarity between the appearance of WD No 560 and that of WD No 307 in 2005, featured on page 109. *V. R. Webster / Kidderminster Railway Museum*

War Department and Overseas Service

Below left:
Delivered new to Longmoor for instructional purposes, WD No 421 (Beyer Peacock 1941), painted in black livery with 14in yellow tender lettering and 12in cabside numerals, was the first large tender engine to work on the Longmoor Military Railway (LMR). Carrying the target for Duty G and the standard LMR goods-train headcode, the locomotive arrives at Longmoor Downs with a train from the Liss direction. Judging by the smokebox-door fittings (which would normally be painted black) WD No 421 has received some Longmoor 'bull'. Whilst on the LMR, in the Corps of Royal Engineers tradition of commemorating generals of earlier times, it was subsequently named *Wolfe*. In October 1941 the locomotive was sent to Crewe and then shipped to Iran (Persia), becoming Iranian State Railways (ISR) No 41.123 and later WD No 70421. In 1951 it was sold to Egyptian State Railways as No 892. *A. Biwandi collection*

Above:

In August 1942 the up mail pauses at Parandak on the Tehran–Ghom section of Iranian State Railways behind ISR Nos 41.177 and 41.180. Following the decision to assist the USSR by opening up a rail link through Iran, the Stanier '8Fs' already built and on loan to the British railways were recalled and prepared for overseas service. This involved the fitting of air-braking equipment, as well as cowcatchers to fend off stray livestock on the tracks. Experience in one of the world's most hostile railway-operating environments soon demonstrated the need for oil-firing, special hot-water injectors and a double cab to provide the crews with a little more protection from the intense daytime heat. The '8Fs' in Iranian service were numbered in the 41.xxx series in order of receipt: Nos 41.100 upwards were coal-fired, while Nos 41.150 upwards burned oil. No 41.177 carries its number in both Western and Arabic numerals, having started life as WD No 437 (Beyer Peacock 1941). The train engine, ISR No 41.180, was originally WD No 442 (also Beyer Peacock 1941). Displaced from Iran by the US Army Transportation Corps, which brought in diesel traction, both locomotives were later shipped to Egypt, where their paths diverged: WD No 437 settled in Italy, ending its career in 1953 with Italian State Railways, whilst WD No 442 returned to the UK in 1948, becoming BR No 48292. *E. J. M. Hayward*

Above:

From January 1941 '8Fs' were shipped under WD control to Egypt, where their numbers were initially increased by 9,000 to avoid duplication with Egyptian State Railways (ESR) locomotives. Later the WD fleet was renumbered into a block 93xx series by renumbering those above 9360 into the gaps, but before completion this scheme was overtaken by a policy decision to renumber all WD locomotives by adding 70,000 to their *original* numbers. No 9359 (North British 1941) is seen in 1944, heading a Lydda–Kantara freight at Rafah (on the Palestine/Egypt border). Formerly WD No 515 (see the smokebox numberplate), the locomotive became No 70515 and was acquired by Israel in 1948. Oil-fired and vacuum-braked, it carries an oil lamp over the buffers in good British tradition. The six-wheel coach coupled next to the tender was the Lydda District Locomotive Superintendent's inspection coach (from which he alighted to take this photograph); this had originated with the ESR in the 1914-18 war and spent its declining years as an office at Qishon Works. *Robin Davies*

Above:
WD No 70573 (Vulcan Foundry 1936, for the LMS as No 8045) stands with a freight at Azzib, north of Haifa, on 13 October 1947. It has been fitted with a turbo-generator (seen ahead of the cab) and a powerful headlight for night operation, as well as stop valves for the top-feed clacks (requiring a larger top-feed casing). The four-wheel brake van behind the tender is typically British, but the stock looks American. In late 1941 the locomotive was requisitioned for war service to become WD No 573 and subsequently ISR No 41.178 and WD No 70573. It was one of the engines selected by Ron Jarvis of the LMS for purchase and repatriation to the UK, returning in 1948 to become BR No 48045. *R. G. Jarvis / Midland Railway Trust*

Left:
In April 1948 23 '8Fs' working within the boundaries of the newly created State of Israel were taken into the stock of Israeli Railways (IR). They continued to be identified by their former WD numbers and were known as Class LMS. No 70513 (North British 1941) is seen taking water at Zikhron Ya'aqov whilst working the inaugural IR train to Hadera on 4 January 1949. The suited gentleman standing by the cylinder is David Remez, Israel's first Minister of Transport. *Stanier 8F Society collection*

Right:

Three of the 23 '8Fs' absorbed by Israeli Railways can be seen in this view of Qishon Works *c*1950. In the foreground an unidentified '8F' is receiving attention whilst No 70308 (North British 1940) and another unidentified example may be observed at the back. Also visible are the boiler and frames of a Baldwin 4-6-0, 'P'-class 4-6-0 No 65, a second Baldwin 4-6-0 and the boiler and frames of a 'USA'-class 0-6-0 tank.
Paul Cotterell collection

Below:

Carrying its 1952 number, WD No 509 *Cpl J. Ross VC* heads a stores train (including tanks) past a tented camp somewhere in the Canal Zone. Note the barbed wire, to deter intruders. Built as WD No 516 (North British 1941), this locomotive worked in Iran before transfer overland to Egypt. In 1956 it was sold to the Egyptian Government, becoming ESR No 832.
Stanier 8F Society collection

Right:
After the War 10 '8Fs' were sold to Iraqi State Railways, and at least one was still in existence at the start of the Allied invasion of Iraq, almost 60 years later. At Shalchiya depot, Baghdad, the breakdown train is being shunted by Iraqi State Railways 'TD'-class No 1427 (Beyer Peacock 1940). Originally WD No 404, the locomotive ran as No 8290 on the LMS until shipped to Iran in 1941. On purchase by Iraqi State Railways it became the latter's No 907 but is seen here with its later number and in lined green livery. Behind the crane is another British tender, from one of the LSWR Adams '0395'-class 0-6-0s sold to the Government and shipped to the Middle East during World War 1. *Basil Roberts*

Above:
Following the disposal of many '8Fs' to Egypt, Italy, Iraq, Britain and Israel the WD continued to maintain a railway-operating presence in the Suez Canal Zone, where responsibility for maintenance and overhaul of the dozen or so serviceable '8Fs' fell to 169 Railway Workshops Company, RE. Several locomotives were named after members of the Corps, mostly after Victoria Cross-holders from the Crimean War; featured here, possibly just after the naming ceremony, is WD No 70320 *Lt W. O. Lennox VC, Royal Engineers*. Delivered as WD No 320 (North British 1940), this locomotive was loaned to the LMS as No 8246 until called up in late 1941 for service in Iran, where it ran as

ISR No 41.108. Later it was one of 59 locomotives remaining in Iran to be recovered overland to Egypt for continued use. By 1952 it had been laid aside and was one of five selected for return to the UK for heavy repairs at Derby Works. Political changes in Egypt ensured the locomotives remained in the UK, all being sent to Longmoor following overhaul. This example retained its name and was repainted in LMR lined blue livery as WD No 501. One of three sold to BR in 1957 for service in Scotland, it was renumbered 48774 (at the end of the '8F' series), the authorities at Derby being unaware of the WD's 1952 renumbering. It was finally withdrawn in 1965. *Stanier 8F Society collection*

Below:
There were several instances of locomotives' swapping identities, possibly in connection with boiler exchanges. ISR No 41.135 was built as WD No 395 (North British 1941) — and still carries this on the smokebox — but became WD No 70321 soon after this photograph was taken at 169 Railway Workshops, Suez, in December 1947. It has just returned from the WD Stores Depot at Quassasim, bringing with it an ex-LMS Armstrong-Whitworth 0-6-0 DE shunter and three 0-4-0 tank engines. *Stewart Currie*

Right:
In 1944/5 15 locomotives recently overhauled at the RE workshops in Egypt and Palestine were shipped for use in northern Italy. Bologna was about as far north as they worked, WD No 70520 (North British 1941) being seen there on 5 October 1945. The '8Fs' were sold to the Italian State Railways (FS) in 1946, No 70520 becoming FS No 737.007 and surviving in Italy until 1953.
Stephenson Locomotive Society collection

Right:
Not all mishaps were accidental. Following World War 2 Egyptian terrorist activities in the British-occupied Canal Zone mounted, and in January 1952 WD No 70574 *C/Sgt P. Leitch VC, Royal Engineers* (Crewe 1937 as LMS No 8019) ran over a mine at Quantara whilst working a freight train. The force of the explosion was sufficient to blow the right-hand driving wheel clean off its axle, whilst on the left-hand side the horns guiding the driving axle were either blown out or had to be cut away in order to remove the wheel and axle so that the locomotive could be recovered to works. It never ran again.
Stanier 8F Society collection

Above:
One of the five engines repatriated from Suez for heavy repairs in 1952 was WD No 511 (Crewe 1937 as LMS No 8021). After WD requisition and service in Iran as WD No 575 and ISR No 41.152 it was laid aside unserviceable and cannibalised until the deteriorating motive-power situation in the Canal Zone prompted its return to the UK. Following repair at Derby and storage at Longmoor (where it was named *Sgt J. Smith VC, Bengal Sappers & Miners*) it was sent north to No 2 Military Port at Cairnryan, on the west coast of

Scotland (later to be joined by WD No 508), where it was used after World War 2 for transporting surplus ordnance for dumping in the Irish Sea. When operations were wound down in 1959 the two locomotives found themselves surplus to requirements, and as BR was not interested in acquiring them both were scrapped. In happier days WD No 511 is seen at Cairnryan on 22 June 1957, fitted with a spark-arrester. Security at Cairnryan ensured that photographs such as this are extremely rare.
Stephenson Locomotive Society collection / Ian M. Coonie

Below:
Locked in a deadly embrace, ISR Nos 41.110 (North British 1941, formerly WD No 389) and 41.107 (North British 1940, formerly WD No 331) have come to grief on the single line between Khorramshahr and Ahwaz in Iran on 2 February 1943. British and American personnel contemplate the situation, but neither engine ever ran again, although both survived until 1946. Their tenders fared better, returning to the UK, where they found new use behind 'Jubilees' Nos 45554 *Ontario* and 45585 *Hyderabad*.
Stanier 8F Society collection

Right:
On 15 September 1951 WD
No 70387 *Cpl W. J. Lendrim VC*
(North British 1941) was derailed by
saboteurs whilst heading a military
stores train at El Zeitiya, about three
miles southwest of Suez. The
derailment occurred on a low
embankment across soft boggy
ground, onto which the engine rolled.
It was not finally re-railed until the
following April; in the meantime an
adjacent siding was converted to a
running line to form a diversion so
that traffic could continue. Here, with
the stricken locomotive still in the
mire, WD No 70516 *Cpl J. Ross VC*
(North British 1941) edges along the
temporary track. A full account
of the re-railing operation appeared in
The Railway Gazette for 13 February
1953. *Stanier 8F Society collection*

Above:

The story of the '8Fs' and the ICI hoppers came together in preservation on 11 November 1995, when, to mark the retirement of the original 1936 vacuum-braked hoppers, No 48151 (Crewe 1942) returned to Tunstead. Here it takes a rake of hoppers under the loading bunkers at Tunstead and towards Great Rocks Junction. Allocated to Northwich from March 1966 until withdrawal in January 1968, it would have been familiar with Tunstead and the

hoppers. Normally only Heaton Mersey- and Northwich-based locomotives were used on such traffic, but for this occasion No 48151 bears a 9D (Buxton) shedplate. Purchased (soon after withdrawal) by Steamtown, Carnforth, because of its good overall condition, the locomotive is now owned by David Smith of the West Coast Railway Company. It has been the most frequent main-line '8F' performer, having visited locations as far apart as Fort William, Scarborough and London. *Stephen Robinson*

Left:

Another view of No 48151 on the hoppers, this time in BR days. Hartford East (CLC) Junctions are triangular and give access to the ICI sidings at Oakleigh. On 2 January 1967 No 48151 storms up the gradient at Hartford East Junction with the 10.16am Tunstead–Oakleigh loaded hoppers. The banker visible at the rear is another Northwich '8F', No 48643. *Stephenson Locomotive Society collection / Alan Wilkinson*

Right:
To celebrate the reopening of the Settle & Carlisle line after extensive track renewal another notable working ran on 19 December 2000, when Railtrack had the final load of new ballast from Ribblehead quarry delivered in the last available vacuum-braked Catfish hoppers, hauled by No 48151! Here the empty hoppers approach Helwith Bridge *en route* from Hellifield to Ribblehead. *Stephen Robinson*

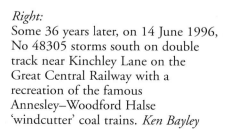

Left:
On the evening of 27 August 1960 Northampton-allocated No 48305 (Crewe 1943) heads south through East Norton towards Market Harborough with a Class E express freight from Colwick to Willesden Sudbury. The signalbox at East Norton, on the ex-GN/LNW joint line between Market Harborough and Bottesford, is of LNWR design (in contrast with the GNR-design 'box at Scalford on page 82). The station had closed as early as 7 December 1953, but a workmen's service from Market Harborough survived until 20 May 1957. *J. Spencer Gilks*

Right:
Some 36 years later, on 14 June 1996, No 48305 storms south on double track near Kinchley Lane on the Great Central Railway with a recreation of the famous Annesley–Woodford Halse 'windcutter' coal trains. *Ken Bayley*

Old Oak Common-allocated No 48431 (Swindon 1944) has been severely checked at Didcot on the up relief line with a long Class F express freight for Acton in 1961. Withdrawn from Bath Green Park in May 1964, this locomotive spent almost eight years at Barry before purchase for preservation on the Keighley & Worth Valley Railway. *Ian Allan Library*

Above:
On Sunday 5 April 1992 No 48431 arrives at Oxenhope on the K&WVR, double-heading with visiting locomotive No 48773. This weekend witnessed the first pairing of '8Fs' since the 'End of Steam' in 1968, No 48773 having undertaken the pilot role the day before. No 48773 arrived on the K&WVR after hauling the 'Lancastrian' railtour between Shrewsbury and Blackburn on 1 February 1992. *Stephen Robinson*

Right:
Rescued from Barry in 1972 for use on the K&WVR, No 48431 represents the Swindon-built '8Fs', with GW-style vacuum ejector; note also the dual lamp-irons. It is seen in October 1993 departing from Goathland with a mixed freight during a visit to the North Yorkshire Moors Railway. *Howard Malham*

Below:
On 24 April 1948, still bearing its former LMS identity, Willesden-allocated No 48624 (Ashford 1943) will probably stop for water at the end of the platform as it returns south through Melton Mowbray (North) *en route* for London with a haul of coal from the South Nottinghamshire Coalfield. Originally more splendid and better equipped than the rival Midland station on the other side of town, the Great Northern station had already started to decay with the loss of glass from the roof. By this time the refreshment room was open only on Tuesdays (market day). Note the signalbox perched on its high stilts. The ex-GN/LNW joint line through Melton closed to passengers in December 1953. A long-term Willesden resident, No 48624 was withdrawn in 1965 and spent the next 16 years at Barry; purchased in 1981 for preservation, it is now nearing completion of restoration at Darley Dale, home of the Peak Railway Society. *Stephenson Locomotive Society collection*

Upper left:
On 10 August 1967 Bolton-allocated No 48773 (North British 1940) crosses the River Ribble and heads north up the 1-in-100 'Long Drag' through Helwith Bridge with the 6L16 10.5am Brindle Heath–Carlisle freight. Note the containers loaded in Hyfits, a practice often employed when the security of the load was important or there was a shortage of Conflats. No 48773 was the only '8F' to gain a yellow stripe on the cabside (albeit applied in error, as the boiler change effected at Crewe Works in 1965 removed the ex-WD clacks which were the reason for the restriction). *Ivo Peters*

Lower left:
Between 1970 and 1992 No 48773 bore the identity of LMS 8233, previously carried whilst on loan to the LMS in 1940/1. Before it could return to the main line a test run was required over a circuitous route between Derby and Sheffield and back. On the outward run on 12 September 1991 the locomotive is seen passing its former home at Toton (December 1940–March 1941) with the 10-coach test train. Its subsequent main-line career, between more regular work on the Severn Valley Railway, has included visits to locations as diverse as Carlisle, York, Newquay and Penzance. *Phil Waterfield*

Above:
Posted overseas from 1941 to 1952, No 48773 began its military service in Iran in December 1941. In 1986 the locomotive was designated as an Official Memorial to the military railwaymen of the Corps of Royal Engineers and is now widely known as a mobile War Memorial. The year 2005 marked two anniversaries — 60 years since the end of World War 2 and 65 years since the locomotive's construction at the North British Locomotive Works in Glasgow. The Stanier 8F Locomotive Society, owners of No 48773 since 1968, decided to commemorate these events by restoring the locomotive as closely as possible to the condition in which it was delivered in 1940. For the second half of 2005 it resumed its original identity as WD No 307 — complete with Westinghouse air pump, air reservoirs and side chains — in which guise it is seen approaching Bewdley Tunnel with the 1.55pm passenger train from Bridgnorth to Kidderminster on 25 June. *Peter Groom*

No 48408 (Swindon 1943) was noted as being at Eastleigh shed from 22 November 1964 until 6 April 1965, while the Engine Record Card reveals that between 24 March and 19 May 1965 it received a Heavy Intermediate overhaul at Eastleigh Works. It was again noted at Eastleigh shed on 23 May; clearly a problem had arisen, for between 2 and 24 June it was back at Eastleigh Works for rectification work. Thereafter a degree of test running was required, and after use on freight workings it was recorded on passenger turns on 16 June. The first sighting was on the 4.12pm service from Southampton Terminus to Bournemouth Central, this being followed by the 6.40pm Bournemouth West–Woking, after which the locomotive retired for the night to Basingstoke MPD. The scene was thus set for two of the most remarkable '8F' workings ever recorded.

On the morning of 17 June 1965 No 48408 worked into Waterloo with nine bogies forming the 8.28am from Basingstoke. At 10.25am the locomotive departed Waterloo for Clapham Yard with the empty stock and then backed light-engine to Nine Elms shed via Queens Road and Goods Yard. From Nine Elms it returned to Waterloo later in the day to work Diagram 265, the 5.9pm to Basingstoke. News of the evening working had spread rapidly, a number of SR staff being on board when departure-time came. Meanwhile, on the footplate, Mark Abbott of Eastleigh Works was on hand to record the following run. (Thanks are due also to Ian Turnbull, for additional information regarding this working.)

Below:
No 48408 and crew stand ready for departure from Waterloo with the 5.9pm to Basingstoke on 17 June 1965. On the left is a 'Warship'-hauled express for Exeter, whilst on the right is a Portsmouth Harbour semi-fast service formed of elderly ex-Southern Railway '4-COR' units.
Mark Abbott

Abridged log of No 48408 on the 5.9pm Waterloo–Basingstoke, 17 June 1965, comprising 10 vehicles (tare weight 319 tons) and driven by Driver E. Hosmer of Eastleigh shed

	Time (pm)	Speed (mph)		Time (pm)	Speed (mph)
Waterloo	5.9½		MP29½		45
Clapham	5.18½		MP31		46
Wimbledon	5.24		MP32		53¾
MP9¼		49¼	Farnborough (arr/dep)	6.0½/6.1¼	
MP11		53½	MP36		48½
Hampton Court Jct	5.30½	58¼	Fleet (arr/dep)	6.7/6.8½	
MP14		61¼	MP38		41¾
MP15		59¼	MP39		45
Hersham		62	Winchfield (arr/dep)	6.14½/6.15¼	
MP21		47	Hook (arr/dep)	6.20½/6.20¾	
MP23¼		52¼	MP45¼		47¾
Woking (arr/dep)	5.43/5.46½		Basingstoke	6.30½	
MP27		40½			

The run of 47¾ miles to Basingstoke, with five intermediate stops and permanent-way slacks at Weybridge and Winchfield, took 81 minutes in the evening peak. (Regular motive power was a Bulleid Light Pacific, which was allowed 78 minutes). From Basingstoke the locomotive worked forward with the 7.6pm vans to Southampton Docks, thereby completing an exceptional couple of days of '8F' activity on SR metals.

Below:
Following arrival at Basingstoke, No 48408 takes water alongside Bulleid 'Merchant Navy' No 35005 *Canadian Pacific*, the latter in charge of a Waterloo–Bournemouth express. *Mark Abbott*

Endpiece

In the kind of scene enjoyed by many but captured by only few, Newton Heath's No 48612 (Ashford 1943) heads away from Newton Heath station with coal for Chadderton power station on 3 April 1965. *Mike Shackleton*